Benjamin Schlesinger is Professor and Co-ordinator of the Social Services and Social Sciences courses at the University of Toronto Faculty of Social Work.   He is the author of The Multi-Problem Family, Poverty in Canada and the United States, The Jewish Family, Families:  A Canadian Perspective, and Family Planning in Canada.

When The One-Parent Family first appeared in 1969,  it was considered 'a concise reference on a strangely neglected topical area [and] essential for research on incomplete families. '
Choice

The third edition of this valuable source-book has been completely revised to update the bibliographic content to the end of 1974 and new essays have been added.

The first section of the book is devoted to three essays by Schlesinger on the one-parent family in Canada,  in Australia, and in Great Britain,  and to a paper by Jetse Sprey dealing with methodological considerations for research in the field. The second part comprises 510 annotations of pertinent materials published up until September 1974,  listed in two parts,  1930-1969, and 1970-74.   The utility of the volume is increased by the inclusion of a complete list of the addresses of the publishers and an author index.   Appendixes contain the latest available census data on Canadian,  American,  and English one-parent families.

# THE ONE-PARENT FAMILY
Perspectives and
Annotated Bibliography THIRD EDITION

BENJAMIN SCHLESINGER

editorial consultant
FLORENCE STRAKHOVSKY

University of Toronto Press
TORONTO AND BUFFALO

© University of Toronto Press 1969, 1970, 1975
Toronto and Buffalo

Third edition, revised, 1975
Printed in Canada

ISBN 0-8020-2171-9
LC 74-599360

"To my way of thinking, the best and surest way of developing generous and idealistic hearts, of giving the community men and women who are well-balanced and conscious of their responsibilities to their country, is to protect the family, for the family— far from opposing the interests of society—is capable of giving to the universe the human beings who are prepared to put justice and truth before their own personal interests."

--His Excellency the late Governor General of Canada, General Georges P. Vanier, P.C., D.S.O., M.C., C.D., on opening the Canadian Conference on the Family held in Ottawa, June 7, 1964.

# INTRODUCTION

This third edition is extensively revised, and the bibliography
on the one-parent family has been brought up to the beginning of
1975. The first part consists of four essays, of which three are
new and written by the author. The papers deal with one-parent
families in Canada, Australia, and Great Britain.

The essay by Jetse Sprey which appeared in previous edi-
tions is an analysis of methodological considerations for research
related to the single-parent family.

The second part, consisting of 535 annotations of published
material through January 1, 1975, covers various aspects of
the family cycle.

One-parent families are not born; they are formed, after
marriage and subsequent family life, or in the case of the unmarried mother, after an illegitimate birth. Thus we see the
cycle among many North American families as follows:

Marriage ⟶ Family Life

Remarriage ⟵ One-Parent Family

This is the rationale for the inclusion in this bibliography of
references related to various aspects of the family cycle.

The Appendix contains the latest available Census data
related to Canadian, American and British one-parent families.
I have also included a complete list of addresses of publishers,
and an author index.

I would like to thank my Dean, Professor Albert Rose, for
his continued encouragement, in allowing me time to work on
this publication. Gwen Peroni, Muriel Allan, Sadie Gerridzen,
and Dorothy Jenkins helped with the typing and editing. A

special thanks to R.I.K. Davidson, Social Science Editor at the University of Toronto Press, for his friendship and help related to this book.

Benjamin Schlesinger

# CONTENTS

THE ONE-PARENT FAMILY

PERSPECTIVES AND ANNOTATED BIBLIOGRAPHY

# THE ONE-PARENT FAMILIES IN CANADA

Benjamin Schlesinger

The one-parent family is not a new phenomenon. Undoubtedly it has existed as long as the human family and probably throughout history has been exposed to greater hardships than the two-parent family. But I should stress at the outset that it is not to be suggested that all one-parent families have serious problems; nor should this group of families be viewed as a "problem." It would be a disaster if we should seem to endorse any notion that the one-parent family is an oddity, a special problem per se, or a group to be looked down on.

While child care and household management are frequently mentioned as potential problem areas for the sole parent, they may well be overwhelming for the lone male parent. Indeed the father of young children may conclude that, in the absence of adequate community services, the obstacles to maintaining the home without his wife are insurmountable. Ironically, he may find that society is willing to provide substitute care for his children (a foster home), but is unable to provide supplementary care (a housekeeper and/or day care) which would enable him to carry on as a full-time father. Perhaps the decline of the extended family represents a greater loss for the one-parent family than it does for the two-parent family in that the former may be more likely to need the kinds of help and support which might be available from relatives in the home.

Prejudice on the part of landlords and employers, loneliness, social isolation, perhaps a reflection of community attitudes, are reported by some sole parents, especially unmarried mothers. As well, the absence of adult male models for boys in fatherless homes is of concern to many mothers.

It has been suggested that there is a serious gap in community services related to the need for many parents for help at the time of a divorce, separation, or desertion -- help not geared to a reconciliation, unless that were indicated, but rather to assisting them to understand and deal with the practical realities of the situation and with their emotions. It is believed that a parent's ability to cope with new demands and to make a satisfactory adjustment to such difficulties as have been mentioned -- and there are others -- could be enhanced with appropriate help at the right time.

According to the 1971 census, we had a total of 5,070,685 families in Canada. Of these, 100,680 families had a one-parent male head and 378,065 families had a one-parent female head. Thus 9.44 per cent of all Canadian families are headed by one parent only (nearly every tenth family).

We can classify such parents into four categories: widowed, divorced, separated, and the unmarried mother who keeps her child. The 1971 census data are shown in Table 1.

TABLE 1
Categories and numbers
of single parents, 1971

| | Male | Female | |
|---|---|---|---|
| Widowed | 38,070 | 184,555 | 222,625 |
| Divorced | 11,260 | 46,615 | 57,880 |
| Separated | 38,845 | 122,450 | 161,295 |
| Never married | 12,505 | 24,445 | 36,945 |
| Total | 100,680 | 378,065 | 478,745 |

The Widow

Quite often the widow is unprepared for sudden death. A period of grief and mourning is followed by her having to realize that she is now head of the family and faces economic and social change which may be frightening. As one widow stated: "I found managing the household finances difficult, as my husband had looked after them. Household repairs were another problem. I had difficulty deciding if I was making the right decisions as we had always decided everything together. I relied completely on my husband. We did everything together. Suddenly I had to do everything alone."

4

Emotionally, the first and most intense feeling is loneliness: "I still haven't got used to it. You can be alone in a big crowd. However, I am now beginning to come out of it."

Another widow echoes this feeling of emotional loss: "The most difficult problem was loneliness -- living in the house alone without him. I was very upset, and although I was a very healthy woman, I lost weight and my blood count went way down for the first six months after his death. I was just dumb. I didn't even realize I was sick."

Other adjustments have to be made because of the changing financial situation of the family. Some widows have to move in with their own parents. "Coming back to my parents' home made life most difficult. They tended to pity me and be angry about my predicament. You get used to thinking and saying 'we' ... and it was hard to say merely 'I' again. This took some time. Income is not a problem because I earn nearly as much as my husband did before he died. I only have to pay a small amount toward housekeeping expenses. Loneliness was a real problem, with other people trying to be kind only making things worse."

Pity on the part of many well-meaning persons can drive a widowed parent into apathy, despair, and isolation. Society can accept the widow and look upon her as the poor unfortunate mother left alone with her children. Usually a widow would prefer a less gloomy approach to her situation and would prefer not to be the companion to married women who have been left at home for a few days while their "husbands are away on business."

If the late husband has provided well for them, the widowed one-parent family is able to manage quite well. In too many cases, though, inadequate preparations have been made and thus the widow has to assume a full time position in order to help her family.

Divorce

In most cases of divorce there has been adequate warning or even preparation that a one-parent family will develop. During the waiting period there may be a separation and children are frequently involved in the quarrels, discriminations, and accusations of the parents. The parents often use the children as pawns in their own need to hurt or to revenge.

After the separation, the children in divorced families face difficulties such as the question of visitation, dual loyalties, and frequently two families if the other parent has remarried. When a divorced one-parent mother has to work full-time to support her family, the children become acutely aware of losing her companionship. One mother sums this up: "The children try to cram everything into the evenings. They are always so happy when it's Saturday and I'm home."

The divorcee, as a one-parent head of the family, finds herself an easy sexual prey. One mother stated: "You can find the odd man you can trust." The stereotype of a divorcee in our society is that she is an easy target for sexual advances, and that it is safe to approach her since she has broken all former marital ties.

The divorced mother finds that in her social life it is the wives who fear her most. One divorcee said: "When I enter a social gathering, I feel that instinctively the wives hold onto the arms of their husbands as if to protect them from the she-devil."

Separation

In the separated family a leading factor of separation is marital discord over financial matters. Very often one partner feels the spouse is immature in dealing with Money. Low earnings, poor money management, exorbitant credit buying, and other similar inadequacies are all examples of reasons given for incompatibility.

The separated woman finds herself in a vacuum as far as our society is concerned. In her social life, most separated mothers feel uncomfortable because they are neither single nor married nor legally free to marry again: "I am in an anomalous position; I don't belong to anybody; I am a social misfit. It weighs heavily against meeting anyone with a view to re-marriage. I am not anything. I am just a woman that is not living with her husband. The separation paper is not worth anything -- only an agreement. I would like to be finished and be free of him. I am nowhere and I don't see getting out of it. He does not want a divorce; he does not want to remarry."

The parent who remains in the home tends to have feelings of hostility, guilt, and confusion. Many wives find it difficult to understand why they must remain in the home while their husband can just walk away. For this reason many separated mothers seek work to find some satisfaction outside the home; for many others it is financially necessary.

The children in separated homes are usually unprepared for the separation when it occurs. Although they are almost always aware of a strain in the home, most parents fail to explain the separation to the children before it happens. It is understandable, then, that most of this group of one-parent heads find that the children are negatively affected by the separation. Most of the separated group find difficulty in explaining the separation to the children and in handling the questions and attitudes about the absent parent. This causes the children to experience confusion about the absent parent, difficulty in school, and to experience health difficulties. Many of these children feel humiliated at being abandoned by their parent. The fact that most of them do not know the reason for the separation adds to their anxieties, and they become embarrassed when asked about their absent parent.

## The Unmarried Mother and Her Child

Although it is nearly impossible to determine how many unmarried mothers keep their babies, it has been estimated that one-half of the girls who are seen at Canadian social agencies are keeping their children. Again, we have no way of knowing what percentage of all unmarried mothers keep their babies.

The single girl who does keep her child is aware that her decision is socially rebellious and violates traditional norms and conventions. The feelings of isolation and rejection are acute. She is separated from society, split off from the "acceptable" or "in" group, with little hope of ever gaining acceptance again. The low sense of self-esteem and despair about being trapped in this status leads some of these girls to impulsive, unsatisfactory marriages.

The life of the single mother is a difficult one. She is a social outcast with few avenues of self-expression or pleasure, and, although the need for satisfaction and affection is great, she has less chance of finding a satisfying relationship with a man. Dating leads to such discomforting questions as "when do I tell him I have an illegitimate child?" Because of their status, many unwed mothers become suspicious and distrustful, feeling that they are only a physical attraction to men. Some attempt to build an overly moral facade, while others become sexually involved again as if they wish to punish themselves.

Although most unwed mothers are sincerely concerned about the welfare of their children, they are often ill-prepared emotionally to carry out the maternal role. In addition, the necessity of meeting the role requirements of both mother and father not only puts pressure on the mother, but also creates confusion and ambiguity for the child's developing sense of identity. As the child grows older, his self-image may become very negative because of his mother's status and his low sense of security.

## Being a Single Parent

When a marriage has ended, whether by death, separation, desertion, or divorce, the now-single parent must face a complete reorientation in this life. He or she now makes all major decisions, virtually on his or her own, with no partner to present another viewpoint. A woman may have great financial problems. Many young husbands fail to provide sufficient life insurance protection; consequently, the widow must care for herself, her children, and the household on a less-than-adequate budget. Most divorcees have to stretch a meagre child-support cheque beyond its breaking point. In this stage of affairs, the woman must make a decision about returning to work. Can she provide a loving mother substitute for her child during those hours she will be on the job? Should she try to wait until all the children are in school? In addition to the financial aspect, many women prefer holding a job for the increased contacts and satisfaction it offers, while for others the daily domestic routine is sufficiently fulfilling.

Divorced persons feel a strong sense of failure and shame of having fallen short of what so many people successfully attain. The widowed persons experience an engulfing grief and loss that even close family members cannot fully understand. Parents without partners must struggle with these enormous personal difficulties and must also be a stabilizing influence for their children.

And what of the children?  When the marriage has ended, what kinds of adjustments must they make?  Parents without partners list their children's fear of being different, of being left out of the main stream, as the largest problem.  Many children cannot communicate their deep anxieties even to their parents.  For those who retreat into themselves and brood, the parents have to work very hard to bring them back to full participation in school, clubs, sports, or any group activities that will de-emphasize the children's difference from their peer group.

Because some children feel the difference so keenly, they are anxious for their parent to remarry, so that they, too, can be part of a two-parent family.  Often they will pressure the parent with such obvious remarks as "Is he going to be my new daddy?"

Despite their uncertain not-married-and-not-unmarried status, the one-parent heads of families are usually conscientious parents striving to bring their children to healthy maturity with as much capability for finding happiness as if they had both father and mother in an intact family.  Their job is lonely and endless.  It goes on twenty-four hours a day and requires countless decisions, large and small.  Seldom is there anyone from whom single parents can expect moral and emotional support, advice, encouragement, praise, or even fault finding.  Isolation from normal community life to some degree is the fate of parents without partners -- whether they are divorced mothers who have custody of their children, fathers who are struggling to build normal relations with their children when they have visitation privileges only a few hours a month, or widows or widowers with children.  They don't seem to fit any of the normal social patterns.  They are the self-styled "fifth wheels" of society.

## Some Recent Findings

Since 1970, there has been some deeper interest in the Canadian one-parent family:  reports by Guyatt (1971) and the Canadian Council on Social Development (1971) brought the plight of such families to the public.

# THE GUYATT STUDY

The study by Guyatt (1971) was sponsored by the Vanier Institute of the Family, which focuses on research, communication and education, and social action. The Institute does its work by gathering information about the family, stimulating research into aspects of the family of which little is known, and informing Canadians of those things that tend to strengthen the family and improve the quality of family life. The Institute provides a forum across Canada for all groups concerned with the family. It conducts seminars and consultations on family problems and programs that bring together for discussion the leaders in a variety of professions and fields of interest including health, education, law, social welfare, town planning, religion, sociology, economics, demography, industry, labor, youth, and parents. Whenever appropriate, the Institute endeavours to influence public policy to ensure consideration of the effects of such policy on families.

Guyatt's study was primarily an exploratory one which included a review of relevant Canadian literature and research, a description of the total population of one-parent families in Canada, an examination of organizations which provide services to these families, and the self-help groups composed of single parents. The findings and recommendations of her study were:

1. The financial need of one-parent families is their greatest problem, followed by their social need, i.e., their need to be included in community life. More adequate public support in the form of a guaranteed annual income and/or a greatly increased family allowance to single mothers with dependent children is recommended. In addition, there is need for a revision of tax laws to permit the cost of supplementary child care to be deducted from taxable income.

2. Society at large is unaware of the problems of one-parent families. There is a great need to educate the public. Only an aware public can make the changes necessary to keep single parents and their children in the mainstream of life, and so prevent their isolation and unjust segregation.

3. Subsidized day-care services are particularly needed by one-parent families with young children, e.g., unmarried mothers and deserted wives, and would be of assistance to most

10

one-parent families if they are to become, or continue to be, self-supporting.

4. Services to one-parent families should not be provided separately in most instances. One-parent families should be served by the same agencies that serve two-parent families because their needs for the most part are identical though frequently more acute. The present policy, adopted by most agencies, of giving priority for service to one-parent families should continue and all services to families should be extended and made more accessible.

5. There is a great need for the standardization of information and data collection by all levels of government. At the time of this survey it was impossible to collect statistics on a national level to provide a true picture of the size of the population of one-parent families now receiving or requiring public support. Adequate social programs to meet the needs of these families cannot be developed unless the size and other characteristics of the group to be served are known. Surely some agreement could be reached between and within provinces to overcome this difficulty.

6. The need for measures to prevent families from breaking down is great. Suggested are more income support for families, more counselling services, including premarital counselling groups and volunteer programs to bring supportive casework services to needy families, and the development of family life education programs in the schools and other institutions throughout the community. With particular regard to the increasing number of illegitimate pregnancies among young girls, there is great need for sex education in the schools, community birth control clinics, and the provision of contraceptives either freely or at low cost.

7. Concerning unmarried mothers, the survey has shown that although unmarried mothers form the smallest category of female-led one-parent families, this category is the one about which the most is known and upon which the most emphasis has been placed in the provision of services and the conduct of research. The survey indicates that the proportion of unwed girls who are keeping their babies is increasing and, although it is difficult to establish an exact figure, may be currently as large as 50 per cent. Consequently, there is a need to revamp

11

services for unmarried mothers to provide help in the way of accommodation, counselling and rehabilitation services to those who keep their children, as we have done in the past for those who gave them up. The danger is that if we do not take the necessary social action these mothers and their children will become locked into the poverty cycle, and many of these children will require the protection services of the children's aid societies.

8. Rehabilitation programs to assist single parents who wish to become self-supporting should be more realistic and helpful. A single parent should not lose either money in the amount of living allowance received or other benefits such as medical and hospital insurance and dental services for their children in order to train under the Canada Manpower Training program. Full financial support (including the additional costs for clothing, transportation, and child care) and other benefits should be continued in order to encourage these parents to undertake vocational training if they feel it would benefit their family. Canada Manpower courses should be extended beyond the one-year limit if this is necessary to rehabilitate a single parent. In addition, the provision of day-care services is an essential part of a rehabilitation program.

Among her other recommendations were the ones which related to the need of organizations such as the Vanier Institute of the Family and other national organizations concerned with the welfare of the Canadian family to join together to inform the public of the needs of one-parent families so as to effect necessary changes in government policies and community services affecting them; e.g., provision of day care services, increased family allowances, change in tax laws, etc.

Guyatt also brought out the need for an information centre which would store or have access to the data collected by all fact-collecting organizations concerning the family in Canada. This centre would serve as a resource for researchers, for governments, and for individuals and groups interested in both one- and two-parent Canadian families.

Guyatt comments at the end of her report: "Little has been written and relatively little research has been conducted about the one-parent family in Canada. However, the recent publicity awarded the investigations of the Royal Commission on the

Status of Women in Canada and the Special Senate Committee on Poverty has spotlighted the plight of most one-parent families. A brief review of the literature on one-parent families in the United States and Great Britain has indicated that the situation of one-parent families in those countries is similar to that of Canadian one-parent families." (Guyatt, 1971, 108)

## CANADIAN COUNCIL ON SOCIAL DEVELOPMENT STUDY

The second study, that by the Canadian Council on Social Development (1971), was primarily an investigation of the lives of 113 heads of one-parent families, and included 44 consultations with representatives of departments and organizations that are serving one-parent families. The interviews took place in the spring and summer of 1971. The project was financed through the Welfare Grants program of the Department of National Health and Welfare. The report is fully illustrated with case histories of the one-parent families under study.

The findings and recommendations take up eight pages of the report (Canadian Council on Social Development, 1971, V-XII). Since many of these duplicate those of Guyatt's (1971), we will only select those which add to the discussion.

Employment It was recommended that wages for women be the same as for men, as is the case in the majority of provinces, and that the rates of minimum wages be adjusted realistically in relation to the cost of living.

Another recommendation was that labour unions and professional associations take steps to ensure that women are afforded equal opportunities with men to earn an income based on ability, and to advance with men according to demonstrated capacities.

Training and Education The report suggested that a woman who is a sole parent should be free to choose between remaining at home on social assistance and joining the labour force, and that in either case she might need to upgrade her competence and to have access to community services to aid her in her role as a sole parent.

The author also felt that post-secondary education, including university, be open to parents on social assistance as well as to others, wherever there are reasonably good prospects of eventual independence, without prejudice to their status as recipients of social assistance.

Among new avenues of training, the need for greater efforts to develop new or greatly extended career lines with substantial extensions of training programs in such vocations as child care, homemaker services, and aides to medical, teaching, and social work personnel were indicated.

Legal Procedures  Great emphasis was put on awarding custody. It was recommended that in awarding custody more attention be given to the welfare of the children and that appeal mechanisms be established whereby the rights of the children may be protected more adequately.

Institutions such as family courts and all community organizations serving one-parent families, including sole-parent groups, should recognize the significance of access to children, and that through counselling, group discussions, and other methods they endeavour to prepare separated parents for use of access in the best interests of the children.

The investigators questioned the usefulness of the adversary concept in settling the issues of divorce and separation because they believed that this concept often works to the detriment of the children involved and can be demeaning to parents. They also recommended to the legal profession that they collaborate with other disciplines to develop new mechanisms which will better serve all of those concerned.

Concern was also expressed about the repeated comments of sole parents that family courts are overwhelmed by the pressure of the demands upon them, that there is failure apparently in many cases to obtain dependable financial settlements from the absent parent, that maintenance orders are infrequently enforced, and that maintenance is not often commensurate with the needs of the children.

Day Care  Day care of children was identified by many parents as the most crucial community service needed by one-parent families. The study found that parents greatly appreciate the opportunities for child development wherever these opportunities are now available through day care of children. In addition, one found widespread anxiety and restriction of the opportunities of both parents and children because of the limited provision of group day care, family day care, and lunch hour, after-four, and holiday supervision.

Big Brothers and Big Sisters Associations   Many sole parents of older children believe that their children are helped or could be helped outside their own family by adults who are prepared to take an interest in them on a regular and long-term basis, thus partially compensating for the loss of a parent.

Family Life Education   Parents were strongly supportive of the recent development of high school courses on family life. Two areas in which parents expressed a need for extension of their own knowledge and competence were those on their legal rights as spouses and parents and on their responsibilities as parents in the sex education of their children.

The Network of Services   The study discovered that a few parents knew how to find their way through the network of services in cities, though many did not.   Community services such as day care and homemaker services, while they are important to two-parent families, are often crucial to the one-parent family, and a gap at such a point in the network of services is more damaging to one-parent families.

Help to Newly Separated Parents   Much evidence was found that the period immediately following separation may be an extremely stressful one for many parents.   Among those who participated in the inquiry, many recalled feelings of bewilderment, grief, anxiety, loss of self-esteem, and helplessness. The presence or absence of emotional support and practical advice and guidance was not infrequently mentioned as making a considerable difference in the individual's capacity to cope with the many demands associated with achieving an early and satisfactory adaptation to the role of sole parent, including the ability to plan in the best interests of the children.   The experiences of many parents led them to conclude that far too often existing services and institutions tend to want newly separated parents to involve themselves in an attempt to re-establish the marriage, rather than to assist them in adjusting to the reality of separation.

Central Organization of Sole Parents   The inquiry did not clearly reveal interest, or lack of interest, in a national association of local groups of sole parents.   There were expressions of need for a centre of information and for a consultative service

15

that could be called upon, for instance, when a local organization of sole parents is being launched.

The authors concluded their report by stating: "One can only re-emphasize the great variety of one-parent families and urge all Canadians to lay aside their stereotypes and to recognize the emergence of a variety of family lifestyles. We believe that in this Inquiry we have been talking to men and women whose experiences have left them with sharp perceptions of themselves, of other people, and of society as a whole. They have talents for enriching their own lives and those of others through community relationships. Only a few of them are active as citizens in their community; others have not found a way to participate. There is a massive job ahead to find those parents who have unused potential for making their communities better for their families, and their families better for their communities, and to open the way for them to play their full part in community life."

## THE CANADIAN SOLE PARENT SPEAKS

Our Canadian one-parent family heads were able to tell us about themselves when they were interviewed by Lillian Thomson, who did the basic research for the report, The One-Parent Family, published by the Canadian Council on Social Development (1971). We are grateful to the Council for allowing us to reproduce some of the interview material.

When a person becomes a sole parent, how does it feel?
1. After A's wife left him and the children he felt very bitter and depressed. He badly needed a mature person to talk to frequently. He does not know where he would have turned for this kind of support had it not been for one of his brothers, unmarried, who at some sacrifice of his own interests came to live with them.
2. For two years after her husband died, B had a very hard time to adjust. She lost weight and worried a great deal for fear she would need to break up the home. The thought of being separated from the children was terribly distressing to her. Gradually she gained confidence with the help of her doctor and of the nurses and the welfare workers that she knew.

3. C was a young man who had had several years of extremely happy married life. He is quite sure that he and his wife were looked upon by all of their friends as an ideal couple. During one of his absences on business, his wife left, taking the children, with the intention of establishing a permanent relationship with another man. He thought he had lost his children as well as his wife. He says that it was an extremely severe shock and he was not himself for weeks. He could scarcely face the empty hours at home. His work suffered. One of the men in his firm helped him by going out with him after working hours or taking him home for dinner and an evening of companionship. He thought things through and eventually he regained custody of his children.

## What was their experience in their marriages, when both parents were at home?

1. Mrs. D's marriage was unhappy right from the beginning. Her husband was a heavy drinker and got into trouble with the police. He is now serving a sentence. She says that she never has enjoyed that kind of security which you experience when you live with a person whom you trust entirely and who will stand behind you come what may. She deserted her home several times, usually with the youngest child. The social services would find out about her absence through her husband, and since they did not want to place her children (in foster homes) they would insist that she return home. The children have been distressed because of these ups and downs.

2. E is a girl still in her twenties. When she was fifteen she became pregnant. Her parents were very anxious for her to complete Grade 8, which she did. They wanted to have the baby adopted, but she wanted to marry. During that summer she completed elementary school, got married, and had her first child. At present she seems more absorbed in her own emotional problems than in her children. Perhaps she missed so much of her own youth that she has not matured to the point at which she could welcome the responsibilities of motherhood. She may be an example of a young woman who feels cheated out of all the normal carefree life that one expects in the later teens.

17

## What happens to the social and cultural life of sole parents?

1. F is very lonely, especially at night when the children go to bed. There is nothing to do except watch TV and read, and this often amounts to boredom. "Then you start thinking of all you could do if you didn't have the kids, but then you go to cover them up or something and you think it's not so bad to have them with you."

2. A young housewife said that when she and her husband were living together they went out a great deal, and she misses the recreation, especially on weekends. Friday nights are very difficult and so are Sunday afternoons. She doesn't mind Saturday night so much because she is always busy getting the children ready for Sunday school and the time is fully occupied. She has made no friends since her separation. Her women friends are all with their husbands.

3. Mrs. G, the mother of several children, finds that the village in which she lives is an extremely cliquish place. When her husband was alive they went out together about once a week with couples and she misses this social life. She has a feeling of being an extra now and she says that if you want to go to a hotel (for a drink) with another young woman people think it queer. Sometimes she goes to a dance with a girl friend and her husband. There are no women's organizations to join.

4. Mrs. H, who has two children, says her social life has been radically changed. She says that she and her husband seldom went out to large parties and functions of any kind, but they visited other couples and entertained other couples. After separation, this kind of socializing ceased entirely. She noticed that women friends would invite her by saying: "John is going fishing, so come over." ... Most of her friends are now single and in their late twenties. She envies them because they can have holidays away from their ordinary places of work and living and also because if they wish they can invite a man to stay overnight.

## What about raising children in a sole-parent family?

1. Mrs. J is one mother who said that she did not find it especially hard to raise her children as a sole parent. It was not so hard that she ever thought of giving them up. This was because each child had a share of the work and they were all

fairly responsible.

2. Mr. K says that he has had no cause to really worry
about the children. He gets mad  sometimes when he comes
home expecting a meal to be ready and finds that the girls have
goofed off somewhere, but 90 per cent of the time they are
reasonably good about taking responsibility with comparatively
few hassles. The household routine is not strictly organized
except for a few tasks - for example, on Saturday morning the
older daughter does the laundry, but each person is responsible
for his or her ironing.

3. L explained that it has been important to protect her
fourteen-year-old daughter from taking too much responsibility.
She believes that a young girl at this age needs recreation,
and her daughter has been almost too willing to share in the
household responsibility. She is doing well at school.

How does the man who remains the head of a sole-parent
family cope?

1. For Mr. M, deserted and with three small children,
getting homemaker service and day care has been an unusually
serious problem. He had several housekeppers, some of whom
were unsatisfactory and all of whom left him. Subsidized day
care proved to be a better arrangement, even if it meant
getting the children up at five a.m. so that they could be left
at the day care centre downtown before their father went to
work.

2. Another father who was suddenly left a widower with
six children could not find a homemaker. In his city there is
a homemaker service, but his needs did not fit the agency
regulations. The child welfare authorities offered foster home
care for the children but he absolutely, and probably angrily,
refused to have the children separated from him. This father
has held several different jobs but his best and steadiest job
was the one he had at the time of his wife's death. He continued in this job for a few months after his wife died but it was
shift work and one of the shifts was at night. He knew that he
simply couldn't leave the children alone overnight because the
oldest was only 15. He said, "I wasn't going to leave them
alone for love or money." He gave up his job and hasn't had
anything to equal it since. Canada Manpower is good to him and

19

if any job comes up that they think he could handle they call him immediately.

3. The man who had the best arrangement was one who advertised, received twenty-five applications, and employed a very satisfactory housekeeper at $150 a month. Only one (man) found his solution, or at least a partial solution, by going to live with his in-laws after his wife's death. The children are cared for by their grandmother. This father could not afford to pay the full cost of a housekeeper, and although there was a local organization providing subsidized homemaker services, it was not equipped to meet a long-term need. Although the arrangement with the in-laws is the best available, it has disadvantages. It cannot be easy for the children's grandmother to start raising a family again. For the father, social life is restricted in some ways. For example, visits from his own family are not as frequent as they were when he had his own home. In other words, he cannot feel quite at home nor is he altogether happy about this type of home life for the children. Another man entered his boys in a good residential school when his wife died.

A mother who became a sole parent had the following advice to give to other Canadian mothers who might find themselves in the role of sole parent:

1. She would advise any girl to get a trade or training. There are too many who imagine they will never need to support themselves for a single day if once they marry. This is far from reality.

2. She would say to any young woman, "Don't ever run up bills." Perhaps it may be all right to charge for small purchases but it is not all right with larger items.

3. She would say, "Don't be too proud to accept help from people." Her daughters wore hand-me-downs until they got into their teens. Last winter the youngest daughter had her first new coat. She could assure young women that they can regain their independence later on, but there may be a time when they cannot afford any foolish pride about accepting what people offer them.

4. The financial limitations of a sole parent should be fully and carefully explained to the children. It is not enough to say "you can't have this or that." Children will respond to

an honest explanation.

5. Even if the family finances are very limited there is no reason why the children cannot be taught the uses and value of money. She made a practice of taking her daughters to stores where they would carefully examine pieces of meat and other merchandise while their mother explained how to select. In those days, any kind of meat, even the cheapest, was a luxury to them. She taught them how to check prices, one store against the other. As a result, a daughter who is now away at college is making a very good job of managing her limited funds. She taught the children to buy good quality in clothes - the best quality wherever possible - and when the girls were small she always bought a size too big so that they would have three seasons of wear out of any garment.

6. Finally, it is absolutely necessary for a sole parent to know how to cope with loneliness. When she was first widowed and the children were very small she felt that it wouldn't take much to drive her into melancholia. She realized that she must get hold of herself. As far as she is concerned, she finds that contacts with people mean more to her than anything else. She uses her telephone a great deal and she writes many letters to people all over Canada.

The Last Word

We will leave the last word to four Canadian women who are one-parent family heads. Doris Guyatt in her research report (1971) asked them to tell what they thought about single parenthood:

1. "I look forward to the day when people will become more sensible in their attitudes toward us: the men - that we are not weak, sitting ducks; the women - that we are not playgirls living it up, nor huntresses after their husbands. We are simply human beings who have made a human error in choosing a mate. A mistake in judgement. Nothing more. And, when faced with the fact that we have, unwittingly, provided an unhappy, unsuitable environment, we have had the sense and courage to change it."

2. "If our income tax laws were revised to give the single parents a break, we could cope, and perhaps even look forward to a more secure future. We might be able to take a vacation

21

once in a while. (I haven't had one in eight years.) Perhaps buy something <u>new</u>. As it stands now, most of us can't see any hope of any financial security, nor any fund for our children's education. I know I myself have reached a low in discouragement; and one of these days I will add a new experience to my life; I'll go on welfare. I know I'll eat better, wear better clothes; my son's health and dental needs will be met. I personally have experienced situations that prove that our society, i.e., our governments at all levels and their agencies, penalize people like us who try to pay our own way."

3. "I would like to see the pressure taken off of single parents, especially mothers, to go out and work. To my way of thinking they have, if they so desire, a very large and important job right at home. It would be more beneficial to society for them to stay at home and be a real mother to the children as in the end it is the children who lose, not having the security of either parent. However, the way our social system is arranged, one almost has no choice. It happens that we are encouraged by almost all agencies to go out and work. Make more money. Buy, buy, buy. Give lots of material things to your kids and forget all about their emotional needs. For those of us who refuse, we sacrifice even the price of a pair of shoes in order to have a house full of love, and emotional happiness. I think as well there should be some kind of 'Dr. Spock' written just for us, to help us know and understand over questionable periods.

4. "Courts, agencies, etc., are much too slow in coping with the problems of single parents. Help in these cases is usually needed immediately not only because the issue at hand is urgent but because the emotional stability of a single parent at this time is at a dangerous low ebb. Patience and tolerance at this time is very difficult to achieve."

References

Canadian Council on Social Development. The One-Parent Family. Ottawa: Canadian Council on Social Development, October 1971. (55 Parkdale Ave., Ottawa, Ontario, K1Y 1E5).

Guyatt, Doris E.  The One-Parent Family in Canada.  Ottawa:
    Vanier Institute of the Family, April 1971.  (151 Slater
    Street, Ottawa, Ontario, K1P 5H3).

# THE ONE-PARENT FAMILY IN AUSTRALIA

Benjamin Schlesinger

## INTRODUCTION

With increased urbanization and industrialization, Australian family life is experiencing many of the changing family patterns evident in other Commonwealth industrialized nations such as Canada and Britain. Increased mobility, a growing labour force which includes a large percentage of married working women, and an influx of a large number of migrants from Europe, have all contributed to varied disruptions in many areas of family living. It is evident from the Australian statistics that marital separation, extra-nuptial births, divorces and widowhood are all on the increase over the past decade. Thus we face in Australia an increase of one-parent families. About 7.28 per cent of Australian families are in the one-parent family category. (Population in 1970 was 12.551 million.)

One-Parent Studies
The studies which are available are listed in Table I.

TABLE I
STUDIES OF SINGLE-PARENT FAMILIES
IN AUSTRALIA: 1958-1973

| Author | Year of Study | Category of Single Parent | Size of Sample | Location |
|---|---|---|---|---|
| Family Welfare Bureau | 1965 | Single Parents | 37 | Sydney |
| Stevenson et al | 1965 | Single Parents | 20 | Melbourne |
| Henderson et al | 1966 | Single Parents | Survey 4000 | Melbourne |
| Sackville | 1972 | Single Parents | -- | Australia |
| O'Neill & Nairn | 1972 | Single Parents | 54 | Melbourne |
| Aitken - Swan | 1959 | Widows | 184 | Sydney/ Bathurst |
| Dept of Social Services | 1958 | Deserted Wives | 330 | Victoria |
| Council of Social Services | 1967 | Deserted Wives | -- | Queensland |
| Krupinski et al | 1968 | Deserted Wives | 254 | Melbourne |
| Council of Social Service | 1968 | Deserted Wives | 413 | Western Australia |
| Schlesinger | 1973 | Deserted Wives | Statistical | Australia |
| Roberts | 1967 | Unmarried Mothers | 349 | Sydney |
| Shanmugan/ Woods | 1968 | Unmarried Mothers | 100 | Melbourne |
| Watkins | 1970 | Unmarried Mothers | 1 | Sydney |
| Schlesinger | 1973 | Unmarried Mothers | Statistical | Australia |
| Schlesinger | 1973 | Divorced | Statistical | Australia |

It is quite evident that most of the studies were completed during the 1965-1970 period and were primarily done in two urban centres of the Eastern States, namely Sydney and Melbourne. The investigations relied on the survey and questionnaire approach and the samples ranged from one case to 349. This does not include the large Melbourne Poverty study (Henderson et al 1970).

Although all the categories of single-parenthood are represented, there is only one study related to widows, deserted wives and prisoners' wives, and three studies each on unmarried mothers and single parents. It is interesting to compare this output to one-parent family studies in Canada and the United States (Schlesinger, 1970). Only one study, that by Aitken-Swan (1962) included a rural sample and the other four states in Australia have not produced any investigations in this area of family research. The majority of studies have been completed by social workers and sociologists.

REVIEW OF AUSTRALIAN STUDIES

Single Parents - General

The Family Welfare Bureau of Sydney (1965: 39-46) studied 37 families which included 21 deserted, 12 divorced and 4 separated units. On the average these families had been in contact for 2.4 years with social agencies and had on the average three children. What was apparent among these families was that two-thirds of them had insufficient income to meet their basic needs, all had high rental payments, and high hire-purchase schemes. Thirty-eight per cent lived in housing commission flats. The social isolation of these families was noticed as well as a feeling of hostility towards the community at large. One-third of the mothers had established a "de facto" relationship.

In a study of high-rise housing commission flats, Stevenson, Martin and O'Neill (1967) included 20 single-parent units. They found that among the migrant population there existed a high proportion of single-parent families and they stated that "the parents did not make any definite arrangements for the children while they were at work, this was particularly so in the case of the single-parent families" (Stevenson, Martin and O'Neill, 1967: 34). In examining the sample of high-rise tenants, the researchers found that 36 per cent were single parents. The income of the women who headed the families was all under $32 per week.

The large study on poverty in Melbourne by Henderson, Harcourt and Harper (1970) included in their survey single-parent families. One of their conclusions was that the group at greatest risk are the families without fathers. Their estimate is that Melbourne has 15,000 fatherless families. In examining the single-parent families in detail they found that over thirty per cent had an adjusted income of less than $30 per week and were living in poverty. In these 4,000 families there were 8,750 dependent children. A further 14 per cent of families (1,800 families with 3,200 children) had an adjusted weekly income that exceeded the poverty line by less than $6. The authors concluded that "The incidence of poverty among these single-parent units is still substantially higher than in almost any other group in the community" (Henderson, Harcourt and Harper, 1970: 89).

This study also pointed out that the fatherless families are not a homogeneous group. There is variety in education, social background experiences and child rearing patterns and problems. Some had a happily married life, while others had been relieved by the absence of the father. Some were well-housed, others badly housed and paying high rents. The incidence of health problems appeared very high among the fatherless families. What was of importance to many of the families was that relatives and friends helped in times of greatest need. Voluntary social agencies also were involved in helping many of these families.

Only about half of the women were widows and of the rest the largest group consisted of the deserted wives. Many of the wives eventually became recipients of Class A widows' pensions. Only 45 per cent of the fatherless families owned or were buying their homes (compared to 80 per cent of the intact families). As far as employment was concerned the authors found that "the mother who is a family head is not much more likely to go out to work than other mothers but if she does so, she is almost certain to work full time" (Henderson, Harcourt and Harper, 1970: 105).

O'Neill and Nairn (1972) examined a sample of 150 Low Income Families in Melbourne among whom were 54 single-parent families. They document the hopeless situation of these families. Their study is illustrated with case histories. The legal issues related to fatherless families have been described by Sackville (1972). His major emphasis is upon assistance provided to deserted wives and unmarried mothers through the Commonwealth widows' pensions and the various States schemes.

## Widows

In one of the earliest studies in Australia related to single-parent families Aitken-Swan (1962) interviewed 184 widows with dependent children in Sydney and in the two country towns of Bathurst and Grafton. She points out that there is a hierarchy of widows in this country. It runs as follows: The war service widow, the widow of an ex-serviceman who was active overseas, the widow of an ex-serviceman who was not overseas and lastly, civilian widows.

For those widows related to ex-serviceman the pension is larger and without a means test, concessions and allowances are more generous and she has more dignity and higher status in the eyes of the community. By contrast the civilian widow pensioner has little status in terms of money and powerful friends. The community knows little of her problems and as a group, civilian widows have no sentimental appeal. "The widow is called apathetic if she stays at home and she is blamed is she goes to work. Her home is visited and her earnings watched" (Aitken-Swan, 1962: 3). Some of the problems of the widows which were found by the investigators were: inadequate pensions, loneliness, a feeling of rejection and isolation on the part of the community, bringing up children alone, lack of male companionship, especially for the boys and a need for support to talk over plans related to day-by-day living. Many were unaware of social agencies in their community. One of the widows in the sample summarized the position of widows in Australia society when she wrote:

> A widow doesn't want charity: she doesn't want to sit
> back and be kept by the State: she needs to earn all
> she can to boost her ego, and the knowledge that she
> was keeping herself and her children would give her
> that boost. There is so much a widow lacks. She
> needs to efface that sense of being unwanted, of being

28

an "odd man out" in society, and while this is not
a material need, I feel that the first step in its
eradication lies in material independence.

(Aitken-Swan, 1962: 102)

## Family Desertion

According to the Annual Report in 1971 of the Commonwealth
Department of Social Services (1971) there were 47,146 Class
A widows receiving pensions as of June 1971. "Class A" widows
are defined in the Social Services Handbook as a "widow with at
least one eligible child under 16 or student between 16 and 21
in her care".

An analysis of the 47,146 Class A pensioners indicated that
40.3 per cent were widowed, 47.7 per cent deserted, 6.2 per
cent divorced, 4.4 per cent were the wives of husbands who were
in mental hospitals and prisons, and 1.4 per cent were dependent
females. The Annual Report notes that:

Over recent years, the proportion of Class A widows'
pensions granted to deserted wives has grown significantly, and the number of such grants has increased
more rapidly than grants to other categories of
widows. In 1970/71, for the first time, the number
of these grants was higher than for any other category
and amounted to 47.7 per cent of the total. (p. 11)

Over the past sixteen years, we have seen a gradual increase
in family desertion in Australia.

## Victoria

In 1958, the Department of Social Services (1958) completed
a survey of deserted wives granted widows' pensions during
1956-57 in Victoria. In all, 330 cases were examined. The
principal results were:

(a) The more commonly stated reasons for desertion were the
husband's infidelity, mental instability, other conduct constituting constructive desertion, financial and employment
difficulties, and the pregnancy of the pensioner.

(b) 34.5 per cent of the pensioners were under 20 years of age
at marriage.

(c) Nearly one half, 47 per cent, of the pensioners were under
30 years of age at desertion; as 51.3 per cent of the sample

were granted pensions within twelve months of desertion, a large proportion, 37.2 per cent of the total, were still under 30 years of age at grant of pension.

(d) Marriages which were followed by desertion within two years and those lasting less than six years were 9.3 per cent and 37.5 per cent, respectively, of the sample. The median for the period between marriage and desertion was 7.8 years; the mean was 8.3 years.

(e) 10 per cent of husbands were under 20 years and 54.0 per cent were aged between 20 years and 24 years at marriage.

(f) 37.9 per cent of the husbands were under 30 years of age at desertion; 23.3 per cent were aged 30-34 years.

(g) 24.2 per cent of pensioners had one child at grant of pension, 29.4 per cent had two children and 27.0 had three children. The average number of dependent children per pensioner at grant of pension was 2.6.

(h) Children under 6 years, and children aged between 6 and 14 years represented 48.7 per cent and 44.9 per cent, respectively, of the total number of children cared for by the pensioners at the time their pensions were granted.

(i) 23.0 per cent of all children covered by the survey were members of families with two children under 16 years of age at grant of pension; 31.7 per cent were in three-child families and 35.8 per cent were in families with four or more children under 16 at grant of pension.

(j) Pensioners who had given birth to illegitimate children before marriage represented 8.2 per cent of the total. Pensioners who appeared to have had extra-nuptually conceived children amounted to 34.5 per cent of the total.

(k) A high proportion of extra conceptions was evident among pensioners who married when less than 20 years of age. In marriages lasting less than five years, 55.5 per cent of the pensioners appeared to have had extra-nuptually conceived children.

(l) Action for maintenance had been taken by 64.2 per cent of pensioners; of those who took action, 84.5 per cent did so with 12 months of desertion. Practically all pensioners who had obtained maintenance orders received either no payments or very irregular payments.

(m)  83.3 per cent of the pensioners surveyed had maintained
     separate households before desertion whereas only 50.3
     per cent did so after desertion; 60.6 per cent of all pen-
     sioners maintained the same type of residential arrange-
     ments after desertion as they did before, but only 59.6 per
     cent of pensioners maintaining separate households before
     desertion made similar arrangements afterwards.

Queensland
     In 1967, the Council on Social Services of Queensland (1967)
reported on the findings of a "Select Committee on the Problems
of Deserted Wives". They introduce the topic by stating: (p. 7).
     There has been considerable and widespread concern
     about dependent deserted wives. For example, we
     read in Annual Reports of the State Children Department
     (Queensland):
          The social aspect arising from desertion is a
          matter for serious concern (1963).
          The desertion of wives and children by husbands
          is still a matter for grave concern to the Depart-
          ment (1964).
          In genuine and permanent cases of desertion,
          the six months' waiting period after deser-
          tion ... is a worrying time for wives whose
          husbands left them ... (1965).
          The factor most greatly contributing to this
          increase (in the number of children for whom
          assistance was being paid) is desertion by
          fathers ... (1966).
     In June 1966, 901 mothers and their 2,188 children were
receiving family assistance. At the same time it was noted that
1,192 children, in 1966, had to be admitted to the care of the
State Children Department since the fathers deserted and the
mothers were unable to support the family.
     The Queensland study also pointed out:
     We draw attention to the position of the deserted wife
     in Queensland where the State assistance is lower
     than the Special Benefit of the Commonwealth and at
     the same time excludes her from receiving it. Either
     the Queensland Government should abandon State

31

assistance completely and provide a Child's Allowance
as in Victoria, or it should increase the assistance
to a level which is comparable to other States which
provide this assistance. The Commonwealth Department might confer with the Queensland Department
to find ways of providing just and comparable social
security provision for this particular disadvantaged
group. (p. 2).

Among the recommendations made by the Committee, were
the ones dealing with the necessity to study the emotional
problems of deserted families.

## Melbourne

In 1968, Krupinski, Stoller, Harcourts, Kelly and Berkovitch
(1970) studies 254 deserted mothers in Melbourne. Their sample
included mothers who were assisted by the Victorial Department
of Social Welfare and mothers whose children were in day care
centres and mothers who belonged to the "Supporting Mothers
Association", a voluntary self-help organization. The sample
was interviewed by means of a structured questionnaire and they
filled out the "Eysenck Personality Inventory" -- Form A.

The characteristics of their sample indicated a 17-56 year
old range with a median age range of 30-34 years. Eighty-two
per cent of the sample were either Australian born or at least
one partner was Australian born. Sixty-one per cent were
Protestants and thirty-seven per cent Catholics (2 per cent not
stated). Nearly 70 per cent had a secondary education, but not
leaving certificates, and 21 per cent had "primary education or
less only". All lived in the metropolitan area of Melbourne.
The median length of marriage at the time of the desertion was
7.4 years and the median length of time of the desertion was
2.5 years at the time of the interview. The median weekly income was $32-$35. Only 24.4 per cent of the deserted mothers
did not change homes after the desertion. There were 852
children involved in the deserted families (3.4 children per
mother). A total of 39.8 per cent of all the mothers with four
or more children had 64.9 per cent of all the children. Ninety
per cent of the children were living with the mothers. Children
under the age of 15 accounted for 82.6 per cent of all the children
in the sample. The reasons for desertion were irresponsibility,
infidelity, drinking and gambling.

The authors came to the following conclusions:

1. Contrary to expectations, the deserted mothers did not come from predominantly lower occupational strata;

2. The survey showed that marriages between young partners resulted in greater likelihood of desertion;

3. Irrespective of whether the marriage was more or less forced or not, it took a considerable time for it to be dissolved;

4. The financial situation of the deserted mother was clearly unsatisfactory; this applied particularly to those who had to rely on pensions and State assistance;

5. Although the deserted mothers did not seem to suffer from physical illness to a higher degree than their counterparts in the general population, they had, undoubtedly, more neurotic disturbances than other female adults;

6. As there were over 3,000 deserted mothers registered with the Commonwealth Department of Social Services in Victoria and as the average number of children per mother was 3.4, at least 10,000 children were involved in families truncated by desertion;

7. An important observation related to the fact that the children of the deserted mothers left school early, thus indicating the danger of creating a poor achievement group with less opportunities than for the general population.

Western Australia

In 1969, the Council for Social Services in Western Australia (1969) published the findings of its "Committee on Deserted Wives". They reported that in 1969, the Child Welfare Department of Western Australia was responsible for 413 deserted wives and their children.

Following the granting of a Child Welfare Department weekly allowance, the onus is then on the woman to take steps to find her husband, make a complaint in the Summary Relief Court for non-support, and apply for maintenance. In February 1969, the Summary Relief Court was handling three thousand current accounts dealing with Maintenance.

In the event of her not being able to obtain adequate maintenance she can apply for a Civilian Widow's pension after six months of desertion. Again she is expected to sign an Authority

so that the Commonwealth may recover monies from the husband.
If a pension is awarded, it is classed as a Class "A" pension.
If the woman has more than three children she can apply also to
the Child Welfare Department for supplementary aids in addition
to her pension.

The Report states: (p. 4).

Nearly all wives are left destitute as soon as
their husbands do desert them.

Surely it would not be too difficult to devise a
scheme for deserted wives without means to receive
a pension immediately to ensure security, and to
obtain the very necessary "fringe benefits" related
to pensions, such as medical entitlements.

Also, there is certainly no cause for the
Commonwealth to delay six months in awarding a
pension to a woman whose husband has been gaoled
for a period longer than six months. The man is
clearly unable to return to his home even is he
wanted to.

The main factors which emerged from the Committee's
investigation were:

(i) lack of money coming into the home, particularly encoun-
tered when the supporting mother receives no maintenance
or irregular maintenance, or such low amounts of maintenance that it does not cover her family's basic needs even
when State aid is given to supplement to low maintenance
the man might pay;

(ii) the cost to the taxpayer in supporting these families at the
low level at present available from State and Commonwealth;

(iii) the inadequate system of recovering monies from the
deserting men.


## Pensions for Deserted Families

The Commonwealth Widows' Pensions for deserted, fatherless families allow a maximum weekly pension of $30.25 for a
deserted mother and two children (Department of Social Services,
1971).

The Annual Report of the Department of Social Services
(1971) calculated that the average weekly rates of Class A Widows'

pensions in June 1971 were $24.62 excluding supplementary assistance and $25.23 including supplementary assistance.

Side Benefits for Widows' Pensioners*
These differ slightly in the six States of Australia and we shall discuss the situation in Western Australia in 1971.
A woman who is receiving the full Class A pension is able to obtain the following extra benefits in Western Australia:

(a) Medical
Free consultations with general practitioners,
Free public ward accommodation and free specialist treatment in a teaching hospital, and
Free public ward accommodation in a public hospital.
The cost to a non-pensioner, who would have to join the "Hospital Benefit Fund of Western Australia" would be $79.00 annually per family. Under the benefits of the Commonwealth Department of Health Pharmaceutical Benefits, a pensioner would pay fifty cents per prescription ($1.00 for non-pensioner) for the majority of drugs prescribed by physicians. (Department of Health, 1971).

(b) Transportation
Half fare country travel on railways and free metropolitan travel on railways and Metropolitan Transport Trust buses is available to all Social Service Pensioners who qualify for Pensioner Medical Services. Pension identification cards are automatically issued by the Department of Social Services on the grant of pensions and are renewed subsequently in January of each year to eligible pensioners.

(c) Telephone Rentals, Radio and Television Licences
Reduced fees for telephone rental or reduced licences for radio or television are available for pensioners living alone, with another pensioner or with a person on a limited income. In 1971 the annual TV-radio licence was $26.50. The pensioner paid $4. It costs $50 to have a telephone installed, there is no fee reduction for this service, but the pensioner pays only two-thirds of the six-months rental cost of $27.50 ($18.18). There is an additional charge of 4.75 cents per phone call, for which no reduction is available.
*Note: the amounts indicated in this paper change continuously as the government raises the rates year by year.

(d) Education
   (i) School Books – Applications may be made in February
      each year for free school books for children of pen-
      sioners.
   (ii) Correspondence and Technical School Courses – On
      enrolling for a course, a pensioner can apply to the
      enrolling officer for exemption from fees.
(e) Housing
   Pensioners can apply to the State Housing Commission for
   subsidized rentals in public housing units.
   Example: A widow with two children, under the age of 16,
            who is getting a pension of $30.25 per week, would
            pay $5.70 per week for her flat in a State Housing
            project.
   There is, however, a waiting list for accommodation.
(f) Child Endowment
   Child endowment is a universal benefit paid to all Australian
   families. The weekly rates are 50 cents for the oldest child,
   $1.00 for the second, $1.50 for the third, $1.75 for the
   fourth, and $2.00 for the fifth child. These benefits are paid
   until the child is 16 years old. Students in the 16–21 year
   old bracket receive $1.50 per week. Thus a pensioner with
   two children will automatically get $6.00 every 28 days.

Training Scheme for Widow Pensioners

The Department of Labour and National Service (1971) has
instituted a scheme whereby single parent mothers, among
others, can benefit by a training scheme. The maximum time
allotted for this training is 12 months. All tuition, and fares to
and from the training centre are covered, plus an allowance for
books and equipment to a maximum value of $80.00

The Annual Report (Department of Social Services, 1971)
indicated that 1,599 women were in training in Australia and 162
women were waiting for approved courses to become available.
Women with dependent children represented 82 per cent of those
in training.

Unmarried Mothers

Pamela Roberts (1969: 49–59) points out that in 1967 we had
in Australia 17,734 ex-nuptial births of which 10,798 (60.75 per

cent) were to women under the age of 21. In New South Wales during that same year every thirteenth birth was ex-nuptial and of all the mothers who had a baby before their twentieth birthday 28 per cent were unmarried.

The author studied the cases of 349 unmarried mothers at three public hospitals in Sydney in 1969. Sixty per cent (208) of the women opted for adoption of their baby, while 38 per cent (133) chose to keep the baby. Six babied died. In examining the mothers who kept their babies, the investigator found that most of them returned to their families, while the others tended to live on their own or found housekeeping jobs.

The author found that the unmarried mothers required the following services: medical and hospital care, living arrangements, financial support, legal advice, psychiatric consultation and social and spiritual counseling. In many cases where the girl went home with her baby to her own family, the maternal grandmother looked after the child while the mother went to work.

An unmarried mother can obtain Widows' Pension Class A of $23 per week if an affiliation statement to obtain maintenance from the father of the child is made. The waiting list for state housing commission flats in New South Wales at the time of the study was 3.5 years.

In another study Shanmugan and Wood (1970) examined 100 cases of unmarried mothers in a Melbourne hospital in 1968. Seventy of the girls were under the age of 21. Seventy-four girls had known the father of the child for longer than six months before coitus took place and in 24 cases coitus took place with a casual acquaintance. Eighty-six girls had sexual intercourse before the age of 19 and twenty-six before the age of 16. When the authors viewed the family life of these girls, 27 lived in fatherless families and 8 had a stepfather. Only four girls wanted to become pregnant while 39 sought an abortion and failed. When they were queried as to their reasons for not marrying the father of the child, 42 stated that they did not love the father and 29 said that their boyfriend had left when he found her to be pregnant. In fifteen cases the parents objected and in ten situations the father was already married (four had other reasons).

Only sixteen girls intended to keep the baby and eventually fourteen did keep the baby. The authors point out that illegitimate births involve premarital coitus, inadequate contraception, absence of abortion and failure to marry.

The authors suggest that further studies of unmarried mothers could be designed to test three hypotheses concerning the aetiology of illegitimate births. The first is that illegitimate birth is a chance occurrence in a culture which practises premarital coitus but not premarital contraception. The second is that when parental relationship is abnormal so that psychodynamic influences exist in the family it may predispose the daughter to give birth to an illegitimate child. The third hypothesis is that neither society nor the parental relationships are of primary importance but that the girl is emotionally disturbed. In the opinion of the authors the factors determining illegitimate birth vary in individual cases so that the three factors, society's attitudes, the parental relationship and the girl's emotional make-up may all be important.

With the influx of migrants from various parts of Europe, Watkins (1970) examined some of the socio-cultural factors involved in the pregnancy of single Greek migrant girls. She discusses the Greek traditional family patterns, culture, marriage and mores as they apply in Greece, and the consequences of becoming pregnant as a single girl in Australia. The culture conflicts are reviewed in this study.

The statistical trends related to unmarried mothers have been documented by Schlesinger (1973), and it appears that about 50 per cent tend to keep their children, and form the category of single parents known as the unmarried mother and her child. In 1971, 25,269 children were born out of wedlock, that is 9.27 per cent of all live births.

Prisoners' Wives

In Australia, as well as in other countries, we have categories of temporary single-parent families. These include the families of servicemen, mental hospital admissions, long-term hospital hospital admissions and the families of prisoners. The research related to these family units is even more scarce than that related to one-parent families. Anderson (1966, 1967) published the summary of her study, completed in Melbourne in 1965 (Anderson 1965).

The author interviewed 84 prisoners, 59 wives of prisoners

and 12 social agencies active with the families of prisoners. Some of the problems of these families included: finance, many of them were left destitute; and housing, many of the families were paying high rental.

On the family side, family interaction became difficult, on how to manage as a one-parent family. The problem of communication between the wife and her husband was a real one. Contacts with other members of the community ceased in many cases upon the imprisonment of the husband and a feeling of shame and humiliation resulted to the family as a result of his imprisonment. The problems of finance, loneliness, absence of male-head, housing, family interaction and a lack of social services were similar among the families of prisoners to those described previously by one-parent families.

The typical couple in this sample had been married for 8 years and had three children. Loneliness was the worst problem of the wives in the sample. In examining this type of single-parent family, the investigator developed the following family typologies related to this family unit.

(1) Families where good relationships before imprisonment remain unimpaired or where a certain amount of conflict is tolerated.

(2) Families where relationships good before imprisonment, but deteriorate as problems become intensified during imprisonment. Nevertheless marriage will certainly resume.

(3) Families where relationships strained before imprisonment, the experience of imprisonment (or the fact that the crime has come out into the open) brings them together and the marriage may be improved.

(4) Families where relationships strained before imprisonment, prison may bring financial or material difficulties but also may bring psychological relief. Contact is maintained during imprisonment and the marriage is likely to resume as before. Or strained relationships before, little difference financially or materially, contact maintained and marriage will resume as before.

(5) Families where relationships are strained before imprisonment and the separation is a severe crisis materially and emotionally, but the family will remain together because there seems to be no other alternative.

(6)  Families where relationships before imprisonment were
     very strained.  Prison may bring further financial and/or
     psychological stress and the marriage breaks up during im-
     prisonment with little or no likelihood of resuming.  Or it
     may bring relief and the opportunity to break up.
(7)  Families where good relationships before imprisonment
     but little likelihood of resuming.
(8)  Families separated before imprisonment and where there
     was definitely no contact during imprisonment.
(9)  Families where husband/wife in complete disagreement
     about the situation.

                              (Anderson, 1965:  198-199)

CONCLUSIONS

     We have attempted to review existing Australian studies
related to single-parent families.  It is quite evident that this
is a fertile area for further research, especially in the other
States of Australia, outside of Victoria and New South Wales.
We could also benefit by examining the adjustment of one-
parent families in non-metropolitan areas of the large sprawling
continent of Australia.  It appears that this family pattern is on
the increase and would warrant more attention on the part of
sociologists, psychologists, social workers and other professions related to human welfare in Australia.  A publication by
the Australian Council of Social Services (Schlesinger, 1973 a.)
contains some facts and figures about single parent families in
Australia.  The Council has also released a statement related
to Family Policy in Australia (Australian Council of Social
Services, 1972), which includes the broken families.

References

Aitken-Swan, Jean. 1962. Widows in Australia. Sydney:
Australian Council of Social Service.

Anderson, Nancy. 1965. When Father goes to Goal. Melbourne:
Victoria Council of Social Service

--------. 1966. "Prisoner's Families: Part I", The Australian Journal of Social Issues, 2 (Autumn): 32 - 41.

--------. 1967. "Prisoner's Families: Part II", The
Australian Journal of Social Issues, 3 (Fall): 9 - 17.

Australian Council of Social Services. 1972. The Family in
Australia: Towards a National Policy. Sydney.

Council on Social Service of Queensland. 1967. Report on the
Select Committee on the Problems of Deserted Wives.
Brisbane.

Council for Social Services in Western Australia. 1969.
Committee on Deserted Wives. Perth.

Department of Health. 1971. Your Guide to Pharmaceutical
Benefits. Canberra. (Pamphlet).

Department of Labour and National Service. 1971. Employment
Training Scheme. Canberra. (Pamphlet).

Department of Social Services. 1958. A Survey of Deserted
Wives Granted Widows' Pensions in Victoria. Canberra.

--------. 1971. Thirtieth Annual Report 1970-1971. Canberra.

--------. 1971a. Widows' Pensions. Canberra. (Pamphlet).

Family Welfare Bureau Sydney. 1965. "Fatherless Families",
in Australian Association of Social Workers, Ninth Conference Proceedings. Adelaide: 39 - 46.

Henderson, Ronald, Harcourt, Alison, and Harper, R. J. A.
1970. People in Poverty: A Melbourne Survey. Melbourne,
Cheshire.

Krupinski, J., Stoller, A., Harcourt, A., Kelly, E., and
Berkovitch, R. 1970. The Deserted Mother in Victoria.
Melbourne: The Victorian Family Council.

O'Neill, July and Nairn, Rosemary. 1972. The Have Nots: A
Study of 150 Low Income Families. Melbourne: Brother-
hood of St. Laurence.

Roberts, Pamela. 1969. "The Unmarried Mother Who Keeps
Her Child", in Australian Association of Social Workers,
Eleventh National Conference Proceedings. Hobart: 49 - 59.

41

Sackville, Ronald. 1972. Social Welfare for Fatherless Families in Australia. Sydney: Australian Council of Social Service.

Schlesinger, Benjamin. 1970. The One-Parent Family: Perspectives and Annotated Bibliography. Toronto: University of Toronto Press. 2nd edition.

--------. 1973. "Unmarried Mothers in Australia: A Review", Australian Journal of Social Issues, 8 (February), 58 - 70.

--------. 1973a. The Single Parent Family in Australia. Sydney: Australian Council of Social Service.

Shanmugan, N., and Wood, C. 1970. "Unwed Mothers: A Study of 100 Girls in Melbourne, Victoria", The Australian and New Zealand Journal of Sociology, 6 (April).

Stevenson, Ann;, Martin, Elaine, and O'Neill, Judith. 1967. High Living: A Study of Family Life. Melbourne: Melbourne University Press.

Watkins, Glenda. 1971. "The Meaning of Pregnancy to the Single Greek Migrant Girl", Australian Journal of Social Work, 29 (March): 23 - 27.

Addresses

| | |
|---|---|
| Australian Council for Social Services | 99 Liverpool Street, Sydney. P. O. Box 388, P. O. Haymarket, 2000 Australia. |
| Australian Journal of Social Issues | published by Australian Council for Social Services. |
| Australian Social Work | published by Australian Association of Social Workers, c/o Dept. of Social Work, University of Sydney, Sydney, New South Wales, 2006 Australia. |

THE ONE-PARENT FAMILIES IN GREAT BRITAIN:
THE FINER REPORT

Banjamin Schlesinger


INTRODUCTION

The most comprehensive report in the world on one-parent
families was released in Great Britain in July 1974.   The two-
volume 1110 page report entitled Report of the Committee on
One-Parent Families, cost a little over $500,000, began in
1969, and was chaired by Sir Morris Finer.   The committee
met on 78 occasions, and in addition had numerous sub-commit-
tee meetings.   Nearly 170 organizations submitted evidence to
the committee as well as 50 individuals.
     The major terms of reference of the committee, consisting
of thirteen members (9 men and 4 women) was:
     "To examine the nature of any special difficulties which
     the parents of the various kinds of one parent families
     may encounter; the extent to which they can obtain
     financial support when they need it; and the ways in
     which other provisions and facilities are of help to
     them" (p. 1).
Volume one of the Report discusses the making of one-parent
families, family law, social security, the family court, income,
the Guaranteed Maintenance Allowance (GMA), Housing, Employment, Parents and Children, Social Services Support and a
Summary.   Volume two contains twelve appendices, which are
primarily statistical and cover research inquiries, income
maintenance in other European countres, the number of one-
parent families in Great Britain, legal history related to maintenance obligations, the Scottish Law Commission report, matrimonial orders, benefits and allowances for one-parent families, the financial circumstances of one-parent families, and
illustrations of the difficulties of children living in one-parent
families.

## The Number of One-Parent Families

Nearly two-thirds of a million parents are looking after one million children single-handed. Of these, some 400,000 lone mothers are immediately responsible for 720,000 children whose fathers are alive but not living with the family.

Table 1 has a breakdown of these facts:

TABLE 1

ESTIMATE OF NUMBER OF ONE-PARENT FAMILIES WITH DEPENDENT CHILDREN RESULTING FROM ILLEGITIMACY, FACTUAL SEPARATION' DEATH AND DIVORCE: GREAT BRITAIN, 1971

| | Thousands | |
|---|---|---|
| Parent | Number of families | Number of children |
| Female: | | |
| Single ... ... ... ... | 90 | 120 |
| Married ... ... ... ... | 190 | 360 |
| Widowed ... ... ... ... | 120 | 200 |
| Divorced ... ... ... ... | 120 | 240 |
| Sub-total ... ... ... ... | 520 | 920 |
| Male ... ... ... ... | 100 | 160 |
| Total ... ... ... ... | 620 | 1,080 |

Thus nearly one-tenth of all families with dependent children have only one parent at home by reason of death, divorce, separation or births outside marriage (The Canadian census of 1971 indicated that 9.44 p.c. of all families were one-parent families). It is also of interest to note that in 1971, 8.4 per cent of all live births were out of wedlock, about 66,000 births. (In Canada the rate in 1971 was 9 per cent, consisting of 32,693 births.)

## Some findings

Among the findings related to the social and personal life

of one-parent families the following findings stand out:

1.  One of the main personal problems faced by one-parent families is the parents' social isolation, including loneliness.
2.  The frustration of foregoing sexual relations so as to avoid the notice of children and neighbours.
3.  The demand for physical omnipresence of young children without another parent's help.
4.  The children who have to fend for themselves because the sole parent is working, and the children may carry a share of domestic responsibility beyond their capabilities.
5.  Some children may feel different from other children because of a sole-parent family.
6.  Among children of one-parent families there may be proportionately more who show signs of disturbed or delinquent behaviour than among children of two-parent families. They are less likely to do well at school, and tend to leave earlier.

The committee comes to the conclusion that further research is needed on the effects on children in one-parent families. This fact is quite evident in Canada and the United States through a review of the literature in North America.

Recommendations

The report includes 230 recommendations. In this review we can only highlight a selected few of these recommendations.

1.  Imprisonment of maintenance defaulters should be abolished.
2.  The family court should be unified in a system of family law which applies a uniform set of legal rules, derived from a single moral standard and applicable to all citizens.
3.  Estimates of the number of one-parent families in Great Britain should be published regularly.
4.  One-parent families should be entitled to a new social security benefit, called Guaranteed Maintenance Allowance (GMA). It should be available on a non-contributory basis.
5.  Housing is the largest single problem facing one-parent families after financial difficulties. Thus housing needs should be considered by local and central governments.
6.  Lone parents, whether mother or father, should not be obliged by financial pressure to go out to work when they

feel it is in the best interest of the children that they should stay at home.

7.  Employers should be encouraged to offer part-time work to one-parent heads.
8.  The provision for counselling services for lone parents should be encouraged.
9.  Every effort should be made to make social services available more extensively in the evenings and on Saturdays.
10. Expansion is needed in day-care services to children under the age of 5 years.
11. Wherever possible children under the age of three should not be parted from their mothers for long periods.
12. Part-time day care, nursery or playgroup is more suitable than full-time care, unless social need dictates otherwise.
13. Social Services Departments should have responsibility for providing day care services for children of school age.
14. More male staff should be recruited for infant and nursery schools and day nurseries.
15. In designing birth control and family planning policies, special attention should be given to those groups in the population statistically most likely to produce illegitimate children and high rates of marriage breakdown.

It is of interest to this reviewer that in 1971, two Canadian reports on one-parent families -- by Doris Guyatt and the Council on Social Development -- had some recommendations similar to those of the Finer Report. Canadians will find the British report of great significance, and it is hoped that our helping organizations will study this important document in depth and apply some of their findings to the Canadian scene.

References

Finer, Morris, Chairman. Report of the Committee on One-Parent Families. London: Her Majesty's Stationery office, 1974, 2 vols., app. $9.00, can be ordered from: The Government Bookshop, HMSO office, P.O. Box 569, London, SE1 9NH, England.
Schlesinger, Benjamin. The One-Parent Family: Perspectives and Annotated Bibliography. Toronto: University of Toronto Press, 1975, 3rd ed.

46

Guyatt, Doris. *One-Parent Family in Canada*. Ottawa:
    Vanier Institute of the Family, 1971.
Canadian Council on Social Development. *The One-Parent
    Family*. Ottawa, 1971.

# THE STUDY OF SINGLE PARENTHOOD: SOME METHODOLOGICAL CONSIDERATIONS

Jetse Sprey

In a recently published study on adolescence the discussion dealing with the consequences of family breakup is concluded as follows (Rosenberg, 1965, p. 105): "If we return to our original question, 'does the broken home have an effect upon the emotional state of the child?' the best answer would seem to be: it depends." A survey of the extensive literature on the topic of single parenthood[1] seems to bear out this conclusion. Whether or not the absence of one parent affects the remaining family unit, and how, depends on many factors. Some of the most frequently listed factors are: age, number, and sex of the children (Monahan, 1960; Burchinal, 1964; Sterne, 1965); duration of marriage; age of remaining parent at the time of the dissolution; and, finally, social factors such as race, religious affiliation, social class, residence (Kriesberg, et al., 1965; Bernard, 1964), and ethnicity. Furthermore, the specific type of single parenthood—bereavement, divorce, separation, or unwed motherhood—is of great importance. The variety—and often confusion—in findings and approaches has led at least one scholar to conclude that ". . . the concept of the broken home is scientifically unsatisfactory and should be abandoned. It includes too many heterogeneous

---

Reprinted by permission from The Family Life Co-ordinator, XVI (January-April 1967), 29-34.

[1] A complete coverage of the literature is beyond the scope of this paper. Sources mentioned are either immediately relevant to the text or are listed for illustrative purposes only.

conditions having very different psychological effects"
(Bowlby, 1952).

This suggestion goes too far. A survey of research
findings on the single-parenthood phenomenon leaves
little doubt that the simple fact of the absence of one
parent affects family functioning, be it in a wide variety
of ways. The 1960 Census lists a total of 2, 192, 682
single-parent families that contain at least one child under 18 years of age (U.S. Census, 1960). Slightly over
1.8 million of these are female-headed. A comparison
of 1940 and 1960 census data shows an increase of more
than one-third in the total of female-headed one-parent
families. Since this is less than the parallel increase
in intact families, there is no reason to assume that
single parenthood is increasing more rapidly than its
two-parent counterpart. In terms of absolute numbers,
however, the single-parent family, as a category, most
certainly deserves attention.

The aim of this paper is to evaluate the validity of
the single-parent concept. For this purpose a clear definition of this notion encompassing its major empirical
manifestations must be formulated. On the basis of this
conceptualization the question of how the phenomenon can
be studied most fruitfully will be answered.


THE NATURE OF SINGLE PARENTHOOD

The terminology used to identify the single-parent
situation in the research literature is still far from definite. Terms such as "broken homes, " "incomplete
families, " and "single-parent families" often are used
interchangeably. When applied exactly, each of these
denotes a somewhat different situation. The category
"broken homes" by definition excludes the unwed-mother
family, while the latter type is really the only incomplete
one, assuming a situation in which the biological father
is unknown. Sociologically speaking, divorced and bereaved families are not incomplete because the absent
parent still may be a significant reference figure (Marris,
1958). To obtain a maximum degree of clarity the term

"single-parent family" is used. This type of family is defined as an on-going nuclear unit consisting of one parent and at least one dependent child. This definition implies a number of things and requires further elaboration.

In the first place, single parenthood can be conceptualized as an on-going process as well as a final condition. Most published treatments of the phenomenon employ the latter definition. I would like to suggest, however, that it is the conceptualization of single parenthood as an on-going family process that is analytically most useful. It is in this way the event which is the immediate cause of the single-parent situation is logically incorporated in the analysis. The relevance of this crisis-provoking event, to borrow a term from Hill (Hill, 1958), is frequently ignored as a major explanatory factor in the study of single parenthood.

As a condition, the single-parent structure has a few universal characteristics which will affect the on-going family process, regardless of the nature of its origin. These universals are:

(a) The absence of one parent. This fact places a heavier burden upon the remaining one. Not only do the instrumental role obligations of the missing parent have to be fulfilled, but also the emotional ones. Given the reciprocal nature of emotional role behavior, it is highly doubtful that all obligations of that nature can be absorbed by the remaining parent.

(b) The single-parent structure is a minority one in our society, and as such deviates from the statistical norm. One consequence of this is the fact that our society is poorly equipped to deal with the needs of single-parent families. The creation of organizations such as "Parents Without Partners" is symptomatic of this situation. Moreover, the single-parent family is often a temporary condition, disappearing after remarriage. This lack of permanence is to some extent institutionalized, because one of the major solutions to the one-parent situation is remarriage. As long as the intact family is considered the normal and desirable way of rearing children the situation is unlikely to change. Finally, it is not a great leap from an infrequent, often ambiguous, status to a socially stigmatized one. Stigmatization of the single-parent family, and especially of single parents, does occur. One reason for this is probably the presence of some categories considered to be moral deviants, such as unwed mothers and, to a lesser degree, divorced persons. In summary, it must be noted that the considerations brought to bear above are of a conditional rather than a causal nature. Stigma may increase the burden of single parenthood considerably, but does not necessarily have negative effects on family functioning. The same holds true for the absence of one parent in general.

Single parenthood as a process reflects a qualitative change in family living resulting from a specific type of critical event. For instance, the bereaved family results from the death of a parent, the divorced one from a legal marital dissolution, while in the case of unwed motherhood the decision to keep the illegitimate child is the critical factor. None of these events occurs randomly. Certain categories of people are more likely to die than others, while certain types of marriages are prone to maladjustment. The unwed-mother family results from three interrelated events: premarital sexual intercourse, premarital pregnancy and birth, and the decision of the mother—voluntary or not—to keep the child (Young, 1954; Wimperis, 1960; Jones, et al., 1962; Sauber and Rubenstein, 1965). Each of the above events can thus be seen as a family crisis of a very special nature. While the latter differ in kind, the outcome is similar in all instances: a single-parent family structure. [2]

The study of the coping of single-parent family members with the stresses resulting from the absence of a parent can thus be connected theoretically with work done on the more general topic of the management of crises in families. A comparison with the reported studies of Hill, Parad, Rapoport, and others (Hill, 1960; Rapoport

_____

[2]This conceptualization logically includes the unwed mother family. The latter originates after a combination of crisis events.

and Rapoport, 1965; Parad, 1965) will be analytically fruitful. Summing up, as an event in the family process single parenthood is "caused" and subsequently operates as a causal factor itself. The two aspects can only be separated for the sake of analysis, but the distinction is essential for a valid explanation of the observed consequences of the single-parent condition, whatever its inception. In view of this, single parenthood should be studied both as a dependent and an independent variable. A brief elaboration of this point is presented below.

## SINGLE PARENTHOOD
## AS A DEPENDENT VARIABLE

The study of single parenthood as a dependent variable centers by necessity around the nature and the consequences of the crisis-provoking event. The "demography" of the former must deal with those factors responsible for the frequency and distribution of the total category as well as the relative occurrence of each separate type. The analysis will have to go well beyond a study of the statistical factors associated with the occurrence of family breakup and its various manifestations. To illustrate the differences between the major types of crises-provoking events, a brief discussion of each follows.

Death in the family is an event of a very special nature—in contrast to many other crises—because it is irrevocable. Remarriage and further physical contact with the departed parent are impossible, while the image of the deceased is frozen at the time of death. The existing literature in the area of single parenthood contains a good many references to the bereaved family. With a few notable exceptions (Marris, 1958), however, death is dealt with operationally. That is, family dissolution by death is the basis for the categorization of families in a given statistical class. It is clear that even the most careful statistical comparison between a sample of divorced and bereaved families can only conclude that families in these categories differ and at best specify the descriptive nature of these differences. The study of the management of the death of a parent is not aided significantly through the latter types of comparison. To get at the heart of the latter problem comparisons will have to be made between families within the bereaved category itself. Variables such as the place of the family in the family life cycle, degree of rational preparation for death, awareness of the approaching death, and the type and duration of the terminal disease, to mention just a few, must serve as a basis for comparison and analysis.

Divorce is the legal dissolution of a marriage, usually following a more or less protracted stage of marital maladjustment. Frequently the family has already been de facto broken before the issuance of the final decree. In contrast to bereavement, divorce does not exclude the possibility of remarriage between the former partners, and continued contact of some sort is the rule rather than the exception. Any study of single parenthood resulting from divorce that does not incorporate the very specific nature of the relationship between the departed parent and his former family is meaningless. As in the case of the study of management of death, comparisons between differing types of situations within the divorce category will be more fruitful for the study of the impact of this kind of crisis upon the family process than comparisons between divorced and intact families.

The nature of separation as a disruptive event varies very much indeed, a fact which makes this category analytically almost meaningless. The issue of remarriage is lacking while the possibility of contact between the absent parent and his family varies depending on the type and permanency of the separation. A basic distinction must be made between separations of a voluntary and an involuntary nature. As a matter of fact, the simple operational definition of separation as a cause of single parenthood is difficult. How long should a separation last before we can classify the remaining family as a one-parent one? Certain types of separation may be extended but with the duration exactly known in advance, while others may be of an indeterminate nature. It is clear that previous knowledge about the length of separation will be a crucial factor in the explanation of the emotional adjustment of the remaining family members. Under these circumstances it is hardly surprising that most comparative studies of single parenthood have omitted the separation category or incorporated it into another one, such as divorce.

Finally, in the case of the unwed-mother structure no institutionalized family process precedes the onset of the single-parent situation at the time of birth of the first illegitimate child. In concrete situations most families in this category contain more than one illegitimate child,[3] but it is the arrival of the first child—and its adoption—which originates the single-parent family. As stated earlier, there is mounting evidence that the decision of an unwed mother to keep her child—frequently children—is a selective event, socially as well as psychologically. Marriage with the putative father—or one of them—is not excluded, while some degree of contact is also frequently the case. Of all single-parent categories the unwed-mother one lends itself least to a meaningful comparison with intact ones. The specific nature of the crisis-provoking event must be explored by comparisons between unwed mothers who keep their children and those who do not; repeaters and non-repeaters; those who marry the biological father of their children and those who do not, to mention a few relevant analytical dimensions.

In summary, the focus upon the nature of the crisis-provoking event must furnish the answer to the question: To what extent can the nature of a given type of family breakup explain the subsequent family behavior of the

---

[3]For example, during 1965, the total number of registered illegitimate births to mothers over 24 years of age in Cleveland, Ohio, was 534. Of this total 457 children—85.6 percent—were born to mothers with at least one previous illegitimate child. Source: Birth Statistics Resident Births (Cleveland: Division of Health, Bureau of Vital Statistics), Table 2.

members of the resulting single-parent units? The traditional research design in which one-parent families — often of different nature — are compared with intact ones is methodologically irrelevant and will easily lead to misleading generalization. Comparisons between intact and single-parent families are not completely useless, however. Within a clearly defined conceptual frame of reference, for example, that designed to study family crisis, comparisons can be fruitful. The manner in which categories of families cope with the crisis of death can be compared with their handling of chronic illness, but it is clear that the analytical focus has shifted here from the study of single parenthood to that of the management of severe family disturbances.

## SINGLE PARENTHOOD
## AS AN INDEPENDENT VARIABLE

In selecting the single-parent condition as an independent variable the major focus becomes its effect on family process and functioning. Most published research has been directed toward the latter question, while treating the various types of single parenthood as given attributes. In this context the two universal characteristics of the former, the absence of one parent, and the frequent stigmatization of the single-parent status, are two important research dimensions. They must, of course, be combined with other social factors, such as race, class, religion, family size and others, to determine to what extent, and how the functional potentials of the families in question have been impaired.

In contrast to the study of the dependent aspects of single parenthood, here comparisons between categories of intact families and single-parent ones are meaningful. Even more relevant are comparisons between carefully designed samples of single-parent units of different types. To assess the effect of single parenthood upon the socialization process, for instance, a comparison between divorced, bereaved, involuntary separated, and unwed-mother families, can be made while a matched sample of intact families may be utilized as a control.

As was suggested earlier, single parenthood as an independent factor is to be viewed as a condition—that of an incomplete family structure—which results from a number of different events happening to the family process. Its consequences, for instance the absence of the father, can be aggravated, decreased, or neutralized due to the effects of other conditions, such as the availability of funds, relatives, and community services. A study of single parenthood that ignores these conditional factors is meaningless. On the other hand, even more irrelevant is the approach that ignores, or merely operationalizes, the nature of the crisis-provoking event and its implications for the continuing family process.


## THE ANALYSIS OF SINGLE
## PARENTHOOD: FINAL COMMENTS

The conclusion to be drawn from the preceding argument is deceptively simple: The causal explanation of single parenthood should combine the study of the nature of the crisis-provoking event with that of the specific conditional characteristics of the families under consideration. It seems symptomatic of the compartmentalization in social science that this approach has not been followed more frequently. On the topic of bereavement, for example, good studies about the awareness of dying and the meaning of death exist (Glaser and Strauss, 1965; Feifel, 1959), but after the death of the patient, or at best the end of the mourning ritual, the record books are closed. As mentioned earlier, most studies of single parenthood treat death merely as a statistical factor responsible for a given type of single-parent family. The final analysis of the management of parental death in the family is lacking.

It is the conceptualization of single parenthood as an ongoing process that provides a frame of reference within which family process and its subsequent transformation into a single-parent one can be logically integrated. It is clear that within this scheme the possible remarriage of the single parent, and thus the restoration of the intact family unit, also can be handled.

Finally, a comment about the analytical nature of the approach suggested in this paper. In concrete situations single parenthood is not just the absence of a parent, but absence of the father, mother, husband/or wife. Family relations are particularistic in nature in which the loss of a parent becomes a very personal event, rather than the mere elimination of a person performing a given role. The personal dislike frequently associated with family breakup through divorce will play an important part in the future relations between a departed parent and the remaining family, while the grief and loneliness usually associated with bereavement reflects the loss of a very special person. Marris (Marris, 1958; Townsend, 1957) brings this out in his discussion of the stress of widowhood by utilizing Townsend's distinction between desolation and isolation. The former concept denotes the loneliness for someone special, the latter that resulting from the absence of company.

It is considerations of this kind that lead to the occasional assertion—especially by caseworkers and counselors—that categorical statements about single parenthood do not bring us any closer to the "subjective meaning" of widowhood, unwed motherhood, and the like. This kind of claim has a certain surface validity, but is essentially irrelevant and misleading. As such, it warrants a retort. Individual single parents may either hate or grieve for their former spouses, depending on the nature of their loss. But whether they do or not is irrelevant to the scientific explanation of the single-parenthood phenomenon. The symptomatology of grief can, of course, be studied within the context of the bereaved family and the findings produced by this kind of psychological approach may be of great use to the family sociologist investigating bereaved families (Lindemann, 1944). The same holds for the analysis of the alienation process associated with the events leading to divorce. But these instances merely reflect the truism that the scientific study of human behavior is essentially a multi-disciplinary affair. The above cited claim, however, asserts that

certain kinds of human behavior do not lend themselves
to scientific study at all. Marris' usage of the concept
of desolation as indicative of the quality of loneliness experienced by widows demonstrates, however, that quite
personal states of mind can be conceptualized within a
social science frame of reference and subsequently dealt
with. This type of analysis does not negate the uniqueness of the feelings and emotions of individuals, it merely
abstracts certain properties for the purpose of scientific
explanation.


CONCLUSION

   The aim of this paper has been methodological; that
is, focused upon the rationale on which we base our acceptance or rejection of hypotheses or theories. Matters
of a technical and theoretical nature have not been discussed. No sampling designs have been presented, nor
hypotheses formulated, except for illustrative purposes.
Implied in the above definition of methodology is our
focus upon issues of validation rather than those of dis-
covery. In other words, hypotheses, and "insights"
leading to the latter, may be derived from just about any
possible source. The arguments presented in the previous sections are directed toward the validation and
subsequent interpretation of such hypotheses. It is that
aspect of the study of single parenthood that is still most
wanting in rigor.

References

Bernard, Sydney E., Fatherless Families: Their Econ-
    omic and Social Adjustment (Boston: Florence Heller
    Graduate School, Brandeis University, 1964).
Birth Statistics Resident Births (Cleveland: Division of
    Health, Bureau of Vital Statistics), Table 2.
Bowlby, John, Maternal Care and Mental Health (Geneva:
    World Health Organization, 1952), p. 12.

Burchinal, Lee G., "Characteristics of Adolescents from Unbroken, Broken and Reconstructed Families," Journal of Marriage and the Family, XXVI (February 1964), 44-52.

Feifel, Herman, ed., The Meaning of Death (New York: McGraw-Hill, 1959).

Glaser, Barney G., and Anselm L. Strauss, Awareness of Dying (Chicago: Aldine Publishing, 1965).

Hill, Reuben, "Social Stresses on the Family," Social Casework, XXXIX (February-March 1958), 139-150.

Jones, Wyatt C., Henry J. Meyer, and Edgar F. Borgatta, "Social and Psychological Factors in Status Decisions of Unmarried Mothers," Marriage and Family Living, XXIV (August 1962), 224-231.

Kriesberg, Louis, Seymour Bellin, and Helen I. Safa, Fatherless Families: Working Papers (Syracuse: Youth Development Center, University of Syracuse, 1965).

Lindemann, Erich, "Symptomatology and Management of Acute Grief," American Journal of Psychiatry, CI (September 1944), 141-148.

Marris, Peter, Widows and Their Families (London: Routledge and Kegan Paul, 1958), Ch. 2.

Monahan, Thomas P., "Broken Homes by Age of Delinquent Children," The Journal of Social Psychology, LI (May 1960), 387-397.

Parad, Howard J., ed., Crisis Intervention: Selected Readings (New York: Family Service Association of America, 1965).

Rapoport, Robert, and Rhonda Rapoport, "Work and Family in Contemporary Society," American Sociological Review, XXX (June 1965), 381-394.

Rosenberg, Morris, Society and the Adolescent Self-Image (Princeton: Princeton University Press, 1965), p. 105.

Sauber, Mignon, and Elaine Rubenstein, Experiences of the Unwed Mother as a Parent (New York: Community Council of Greater New York, 1965).

Sterne, Richard S., Delinquent Conduct and Broken Homes (New Haven: College and University Press, 1965).

Townsend, Peter, The Family Life of Old People
    (London: Routledge and Kegan Paul, 1957), p. 182.
U.S. Bureau of Census, Population Series, 1960, Final
    Report PC (2)-4A, Families, Tables 3, 6.
Wimperis, Virginia, The Unmarried Mother and Her
    Child (London: George Allen and Unwin, 1960).
Young, Leontine R., Out of Wedlock (New York: McGraw-
    Hill, 1954).

ANNOTATED BIBLIOGRAPHY

MARRIAGE AND FAMILY

ANDREWS, R. O., and H. T. CHRISTENSEN. "Relationship of Absence of a Parent to Courtship Status: A Repeat Study," American Sociological Review, XVI (August 1951), 541-544.
A replication of Winch's study of absence of a parent to courtship behavior. The sample consisted of 1,077 males and 626 females.

ANSHEN, Ruth N., ed. The Family: Its Function and Destiny. New York: Harper and Bros., 1959.
A symposium on the family, containing 24 selections and focusing upon the necessity for man to pursue moral ideals and spiritual and social strength through application of the perspective of science.

BARTEMEIER, Leo. "The Contribution of the Father to the Mental Health of the Family," American Journal of Psychiatry, CX (October 1953), 277-280.
A discussion of the Cornelian Corner, a family agency in Detroit, and some observations about the role of father in family life.

BELL, Robert R. Marriage and Family Interaction. Revised. Homewood: Dorsey Press, 1967.
A "value-free" approach to marriage and family interaction through a heavy emphasis on objective findings of social research in the area of family life.

BELL, Robert R., ed. Studies in Marriage and the Family. New York: Thomas Y. Crowell, 1968.
A summary of eight research studies related to

American marriage from 1938 to 1967.

BELL, Norman W., and Ezra F. VOGEL, eds. A Modern Introduction to the Family. New York: The
Free Press, 1968.
Fifty-two selections of readings on the family from the
structural-functional theoretical framework.

BOALT, Gunnar. Family and Marriage. New York:
David McKay, 1965.
A Swedish social scientist looks at marriage and family
life. Includes some comparative data.

BOSSARD, James H. S., and Eleanor Stoker BOLL.
"Marital Unhappiness in the Life Cycle," Marriage
and Family Living, XVII (February 1955), 10-14.
A study of 440 married persons (215 women and 225
men) who were reared in large families. They were
rated for marital happiness by a brother or a sister.
A considerable amount of unhappiness was found, which
had not yet reached the critical stage of separation, desertion, or divorce.

BOSSARD, James H. S., ed. "Toward Family Stability,"
The Annals, CCLXXII (November 1950), whole issue.
Twenty-four contributors discuss family life, family ad-
justments, family stability, and instability.

BURGESS, Ernest W., and Harvey J. LOCKE. The
Family. 2nd edition. New York: American Book
Company, 1960.
An analysis of the family's transition from institution to
a companionship role in our society.

BURGESS, Ernest W., and Paul WALLIN. Engagement
and Marriage. Chicago: J. B. Lippincott, 1953.
A report on the author's study of engaged couples and a
follow-up after three to five years of marriage. The
study was done during the 1937-43 period. It includes
in a less intensified manner data from other studies in
family life.

BURGESS, Ernest W., and Leonard S. COTTRELL.
   Predicting Success or Failure in Marriage. Englewood Cliffs: Prentice-Hall, 1939.
A report of the extensive research work done by the authors, dealing with the establishment of a validated in-
strument for predicting either the success or failure of
marriage. Sociologically oriented.

CAVAN, Ruth S. The American Family. 3rd edition.
   New York: Thomas Y. Crowell, 1963.
A sociological analysis of the contemporary American
family which takes into account recent research up to
1963 and changes in social conditions that affect families' attitudes and ways of life.

CAVAN, Ruth S., ed. Marriage and Family in the Modern World. 2nd edition. New York: Thomas Y.
   Crowell, 1965.
Seventy-eight articles follow the family life cycle as a
frame of reference. Included are readings on the significance of marriage and the family today, men as earners,
and crises in the family.

CHRISTENSEN, H. T., ed. Handbook of Marriage and
   the Family. Chicago: Rand McNally, 1964.
A compilation of papers which report on the present
state of knowledge in the area of marriage and family,
evaluates methods used in obtaining this knowledge,
spotlights significant gaps, and synthesizes the material
in terms of family theory.

COALE, Ansley J., Lloyd A. FALLERS, Marion J.
   LEVY, Jr., David M. SCHNEIDER, and Silvan S.
   TOMKINS. Aspects of the Analysis of Family
   Structure. Princeton: Princeton University Press,
   1965.
An analysis of the relation between kinship structure and
the family unit from the perspective of sociology, anthro-
pology, psychology, and demography.

CORNELL UNIVERSITY. Men and Family Living.
Ithaca: Department of Child Development and Family Relationships, Extension Department, 1964.
A folder containing documents related to the place of
men in families. An essay by Frederick A. Kunz gives
a background picture of the male role in the home.

COSER, Rose L., ed. The Family: Its Structure and
Functions. New York: St. Martin's Press, 1964.
A selection of 33 articles on the family. The theoretical basis of the book is the view that the family is a
mediator rather than a creator of social values.

DUVALL, Evelyn M. Family Development. 3rd edition.
New York: J. B. Lippincott, 1967.
A study of the nuclear family with emphasis on the fam-
ily cycle.

--------. In-Laws: Pro and Con. New York: Association Press, 1954.
A report and discussion of a research project dealing
with various aspects of in-law relationships.

ENGLISH, O. Spurgeon. "The Psychological Role of
the Father in the Family," Social Casework, XXXV
(October 1964), 323-329.
The author points up the misunderstood and confused
but nonetheless very important role of the father. The
fragmentation of the family because of cultural changes
such as urbanization makes it necessary for the parent
of today to attempt to neutralize the effects of some of
these influences.

--------. "The Psychological Role of the Father in the
Family," in Casework Papers, 1954 (from the National Conference of Social Work). New York: Family Service Association of America, 1955, pp. 18-
30.
This paper emphasizes the importance of the father's
role in the life of a growing young boy or girl. His role
in the family has many facets: he must be husband,

father, member of the workaday world, teacher, mentor, and hero.

ENGLISH, O. Spurgeon, and Constance T. FOSTER.
Fathers Are Parents Too. New York: G. P.
Putnam's Sons, 1951.
The role father plays in the various stages of the growth
cycle of children. A chapter on "Father by Adoption" is
included.

FAMILY MOBILITY IN OUR DYNAMIC SOCIETY. Ames:
Iowa State University Press, 1965.
Consideration is given to family problems and processes
brought about by changing agricultural, economic, and
social conditions. The 15 essays are organized under
headings of societal setting, changing family roles,
problems and adjustments of families who stay and those
who move.

FAMILY SERVICE ASSOCIATION OF AMERICA. The
Significance of the Father. New York, 1959.
Four papers discuss forms of fathering, strengthening
the father's role, and fatherless families in public assistance (2 papers).

FARBER, Bernard. Family: Organization and Interaction. San Francisco: Chandler, 1964.
Concentrates on the explanation of change in the family
with the major focus on the contemporary family in the
United States.

FARBER, Bernard, ed. Kinship and Family Organization. New York: John Wiley and Sons, 1966.
Thirty-six papers emphasize the relation between the
organization of the overall kinship structure and the
characteristics of the nuclear family unit throughout
the family life cycle.

FARBER, Seymour, Piero MUSTACCHI, and Roger H. L.
WILSON, eds. Man and Civilization: The Family's
Search for Survival. New York: McGraw-Hill, 1965.

Twenty-four authorities from various disciplines weigh the impact of a modern industrial society on American family life. The papers reaffirm the indispensability of the family and provide a broad body of facts and interpretations concerning the family's future.

FISHBEIN, Morris, and Ruby Jo Reeves KENNEDY, eds. Modern Marriage and Family Living. New York: Oxford University Press, 1957.
Thirty-seven readings dealing with marriage. Major emphasis is on the social aspects of marriage, preparation for marriage, marital relationships, and children in marriage.

FOOTE, Nelson N., and Leonard S. COTTRELL. Identity and Interpersonal Competence. Chicago: University of Chicago Press, 1955.
Discusses research dealing with the American family between the years 1945 to 1954.

GLICK, Paul C. American Families. New York: John Wiley and Sons, 1957.
A census monograph containing data related to various aspects of family life.

GOODE, William J. The Family. Englewood Cliffs: Prentice-Hall, 1964.
This short book emphasizes the complex relation between family systems and the larger social structure.

HANDEL, Gerald. "Psychological Study of Whole Families," Psychological Bulletin, LXIII (January 1965), 19-41.
Nearly 100 studies related to intact families are reviewed, analyzed, and discussed by the author. Major current approaches and present research methods are examined.

HANDEL, Gerald, ed. The Psychosocial Interior of the Family. Chicago: Aldine, 1967.
Twenty-three selections draw upon findings from many

disciplines to provide a composite view of the whole family and the complex interplay between self and collectivity in family life.

HILL, Reuben. "Social Stresses on the Family," Social
    Casework, XXXIX (February-March 1958), 139-150.
Crisis requires adaptation of existing behavior patterns by all family members in order to meet the demands of the new situation.

HOFFMAN, Lois Wladis. "The Father's Role in the
    Family and the Child's Peer-Group Adjustment,"
    Merrill-Palmer Quarterly, VII (April 1961), 97-
    105.
A study of 445 boys and girls in the elementary schools of Detroit. All are from white, intact families with a socio-economic cross-sectional background. The paper focuses on the father's relationship to his wife and his child.

KENKEL, William F. The Family in Perspective: A
    Fourfold Analysis. 2nd edition. New York:
    Appleton-Century-Crofts, 1966.
This book uses the psychoanalytic approach to family analysis and treats the family in a developmental perspective. Attempts to provide an overview of the "scientific" approach to the study of the family.

KEPHART, William M. The Family, Society, and the
    Individual. 2nd edition. Boston: Houghton-Mifflin,
    1966.
A presentation of the family as a system of interacting personalities and as a social institution sensitive to the structural expectations of society. Interweaves research findings and sociological analysis.

KIRKPATRICK, Clifford. The Family: As Process and
    Institution. 2nd edition. New York: The Ronald
    Press, 1963.
A comprehensive sociology of the family, treating the nature and origins of the family in social context and

the family through its life cycle. Crisis and family reorganization are dealt with in depth.

KLEIN, Ted. The Father's Book. New York: William
    Morrow, 1968.
This guide to men who want to be "better fathers" includes chapters related to absent fathers and divorced
fathers (Chapters VIII and IX, pp. 165-202) as well as
stepfathers (pp. 202-223).

LEE, Alfred McClung, and Elizabeth LEE. Marriage
    and the Family. New York: Barnes and Noble, 1961.
This book summarizes and interprets research findings
on most aspects of family life.

LESLIE, Gerald R. The Family in Social Context.
    London: Oxford University Press, 1967.
A comprehensive up-to-date sociology of the family,
which incorporates cross-cultural, historical,
sociological-institutional, and life cycle material.

LUTZ, Werner A. "Marital Incompatibility," in Social
    Work and Social Problems, edited by Nathan E.
    Cohen. New York: National Association of Social
    Workers, 1964, pp. 41-152.
In this essay dealing with all aspects of marital incompatibility as a social problem the author includes a discussion of current resources and services for dealing
with the problem.

MERRILL-PALMER QUARTERLY, "The Influence of
    the Father in the Family Setting," XI (April 1965),
    whole issue.
Five papers discuss the importance of father in the
nuclear family in America, and most review existing
research studies in this area.

NASH, John. "The Father in Contemporary Culture
    and Current Psychological Literature," Child De-
    velopment, XXXVI (March 1968), 261-297.
A review of 106 studies related to the role and position

of father in the North American family.

NYE, F. Ivan, and Felix M. BERARDO. Emerging
  Conceptual Frameworks in Family Analysis. New
  York: Macmillan, 1966.
Considers eleven "conceptual frameworks" for family
study.

PARSONS, Talcott, and Robert E. BALES. Family,
  Socialization, and Interaction Process. New York:
  The Free Press, 1955.
A theoretical work on the family which has been the
basis of certain theories related to the nuclear family
in America.

RODMAN, Hyman. "Talcott Parson's View of the
  Changing American Family," Merrill-Palmer
  Quarterly, XI (July 1965), 209-228.
An extensive review and analysis of Parson's writings
on the nuclear family in America.

SHANAS, Ethel, and Gordon F. STREIB, eds. Social
  Structure and the Family: Generational Relations.
  Englewood Cliffs: Prentice-Hall, 1965.
Fifteen papers focus on the three-generational family in
America. The authors include sociologists, psycholo-
gists, social workers, economists, and a law professor.

SIMPSON, George. People in Families. New York:
  Thomas Y. Crowell, 1960.
An attempt to integrate the psychoanalytic and sociologi-
cal approaches to the family.

SIRJAMAKI, John. The American Family in the Twentieth Century. Cambridge: Harvard University
  Press, 1953.
An interpretation of the findings of social scientists concerning the American family, including family dissolution.

SPREY, Jetse. "Family Disorganization: Toward a
    Conceptual Clarification," Journal of Marriage and
    the Family, XXVIII (November 1966), 398-406.
A distinction is made between family disorganization and
violation of family role obligations.

STEPHENS, William N., ed. Reflections on Marriage.
    New York: Thomas Y. Crowell, 1968.
Sixteen selections discuss modern marriage, including
the factors necessary in marital adjustment.

STROUP, Atlee L. Marriage and Family: A Develop-
    mental Approach. New York: Appleton-Century-
    Crofts, 1966.
This book assembles and evaluates a great mass of research on marriage and the family and shows how the
parts dovetail.

SUSSMANN, Marvin B., ed. Sourcebook in Marriage
    and the Family. 3rd edition. Boston: Houghton-
    Mifflin, 1968.
Sixty-two papers discuss the family and its problems.

TERMAN, Louis, et al. Psychological Factors in Mar-
    ital Happiness. New York: McGraw-Hill, 1938.
A report of an extensive study on factors in marital
happiness.

UDRY, J. Richard. The Social Context of Marriage.
    New York: J. B. Lippincott, 1966.
A sociology of marriage. In emphasizing the heterosexual relationship it delimits consideration of child
rearing, kinship structures, and other institutional relationships. The author uses the sex pairs as the central focus.

WALLER, Willard. The Family. Revised by Reuben
    Hill. New York: The Dryden Press, 1951.
The book deals with the bargaining and exploitative attitudes in courtship, family disorganization, parenthood,

conflict in marriage, and proposed changes in family designs.

WILLIAMSON, Robert C. Marriage and Family Relations. New York: John Wiley and Sons, 1966.
The author uses an interactionist framework and proceeds on the assumption that marriage and the family cannot be adequately understood apart from other institutions that shape personality. The focus is both psychological and sociological.

WINCH, Robert F. The Modern Family. New York: Holt, Rinehart and Winston, 1963.
Presents a general theory of the family and utilizes this theory in an analysis of the family in the United States.

--------. "The Relation between the Loss of a Parent and Progress in Courtship," Journal of Social Psychology, XXIX (February 1949), 51-56.
The relation of absence of a parent and level of heterosexual involvement is examined in 495 males and 566 native-born white college students in semi-rural midwestern United States.

ZELDITCH, Morris. "Family, Marriage and Kinship," in Handbook of Modern Sociology, edited by Robert E. L. Faris. Chicago: Rand McNally, 1964, pp. 680-733.
A review of the definitions and functions of the family including sections on marriage and divorce.

ONE-PARENT FAMILY

GENERAL

BELL, Robert R. "The One-Parent Mother in the Negro Lower Class," Social Forces, XLIII (May

1965), 493-501.
This study of 194 one-parent mothers examines their parental and marriage roles.

--------. "Lower Class Negro Mothers and Their Children," Integrated Education, II (December-January 1964-1965), 23-27.
Two hundred and two one-parent negro mothers in a lower class neighborhood in Philadelphia were interviewed to ascertain their ambitions for the education of their children.

BERNARD, Sydney E. Fatherless Families: Their Economic and Social Adjustment. Waltham: Brandeis University, Graduate School for Advanced Studies in Social Welfare, 1964.
A study of 80 white women of the lower class who are heads of households, all totally or partially supported by public welfare funds.

BURTON, Roger V., and John W. M. WHITING. "The Absent Father and Cross-Sex Identity," Merrill-Palmer Quarterly, XI (April 1965), 85-96.
This paper contains a review of the literature on the effect of father absence in the household. The authors present findings of a cross-cultural study in this area completed at Harvard University.

CANADA. Dominion Bureau of Statistics. Canadian Families: General Review, 1961 Census. Ottawa, 1967, Bulletin 7.2-1, Catalogue No. 99-526.
A summary of family statistics includes material on one-parent families in Canada.

CARTER, Genevieve W. "The Employment Potential of AFDC Mothers," Welfare in Review, VI (July-August 1968), 1-11.
A discussion of the potential work possibilities of mothers who head families and who are receiving financial

help through the Aid to Families with Dependent Children program (AFDC).

CATHOLIC FAMILY SERVICE, CALGARY. The One Parent Family. Ottawa: Canadian Conference on the Family, 1964.
A study of 30 one-parent families who came to the attention of the agency. Only two parents were men.

DESPERT, Louise. "The Fatherless Family," Child Study, XXIV (Summer 1957), 22-28.
The emotional climate of the family before the father's death or absence greatly affects the child's reaction to such separation.

ENGLESON, Jim, and Janet ENGLESON. Parents without Partners. New York: E. P. Dutton, 1961.
A guide for divorced, widowed, or separated parents, written by a presently married couple, each of whom had been original members of Parents Without Partners, Inc.

ERNEY, Catherine M. "Meeting the Needs of the Fatherless Family," in Casework Papers, 1956 (from the National Conference of Social Work). New York: Family Service Association of America, 1956, pp. 60-70.
Regardless of how the father's absence has come about, various family reactions are inevitable. The paper discusses some of these reactions, ways by which the caseworker can help the family, how far to go in the ego-supportive approach, and various types of intensive treatment of the remaining members of the family.

FREUDENTHAL, Kurt. "The Only Parent," The Single Parent, VIII (December 1965), 10-12.
A discussion of what the parent and child face growing up in a one-parent family.

--------. "Problems of the One-Parent Family,"
    Social Work, IV (January 1959), 44-48.
Aims to identify characteristic problems of the one-
parent family. It is based on material presented in
group discussions among single parents, under the aus-
pices of the Baltimore Department of Education, covering a school year 30-week period continued over five
years.

--------. "A Class for 'Only Parents'," Understanding
    the Child, XXV (October 1956), 111-113.
A discussion of the developments in a class of "only parents" in Baltimore conducted by a professional leader.

GAVAI, Josef E. "Sex and the Single Parent," Sexology,
    XXXIV (October 1967), 148-150.
Sex guidance for the single-parent mother, presenting
the ambivalent sexual feelings of a woman in this position.

--------. "Single Parents and the Sexual Revolution,"
    The Single Parent, X (July 1967), 4-6 and 9.
A psychologist examines the sexual attitudes of single
parents.

GLASSER, Paul, and Elizabeth NAVARRE. "Structural
    Problems of the One-Parent Family," Journal of
    Social Issues, XXI (January 1965), 98-109.
This paper focuses on the task, communication, and af-
fectional structural characteristics of one-parent families in the United States. The authors point to the need
to take into account this situational factor in proposing
policy and practice solutions to the poverty problem.

HILL, Reuben, and Donald A. HANSEN. "Families
    under Stress," in Handbook of Marriage and the
    Family, edited by Harold T. Christensen. Chicago:
    Rand McNally, 1964, pp. 782-822.
An overview of sociological studies in family crises
which includes the one-parent family.

ILGENFRITZ, Marjorie P. "Mothers on Their Own: Widows and Divorcées, " Marriage and Family Living, XXIII (February 1961), 38-41.
With 4, 000, 000 women and 600, 000 men as heads of one-parent families in the U.S.A., the Educational Division of the Guidance Center of New Rochelle in Westchester County, New York, decided to meet local needs by offering a six-session series of discussions entitled "The One-Parent Family." It was led by a professional leader in Parent Education during the spring of 1958. Twelve women attended the full course.

JONES, Eve. Raising Your Child in a Fatherless Home. Glencoe: The Free Press, 1963.
An advice- and support-giving book dealing with the one-parent family.

KOCH, Margaret Body. "Anxiety in Preschool Children from Broken Homes, " Merrill-Palmer Quarterly, VII (October 1961), 225-232.
Twenty-two children ranging in age from 43 months to 67 months were chosen from day nurseries in Columbus, Ohio. The findings indicate that the preschool children from broken homes were more likely to have adjustment difficulties than the children from intact homes.

KRIESBERG, Louis. "Rearing Children for Educational Achievement in Fatherless Families, " Journal of Marriage and the Family, XXIX (May 1967), 288-301.
The investigator interviewed 1, 274 respondents in four Syracuse, New York, public housing projects, two of which were in the middle-income neighborhoods. The findings indicate that husbandless mothers are generally more concerned about the educational achievement of their children than are married mothers.

KRIESBERG, Louis, and Seymour S. BELLIN. Fatherless Families and Housing. Syracuse: Syracuse University Youth Development Center, 1965.

A study of 129 one-parent families in four public housing projects in Syracuse. Personally conducted interviews were used to obtain the data.

LANDIS, Paul H. The Broken Home In Teen-age Adjustments. Washington: State College of Washington, 1953, Bulletin #542.
A study of 4,394 graduating high school seniors in 1947 of whom 20 percent were in broken families. The author discusses the composition and life of the teen-agers in these broken families in the state of Washington.

LANGNER, Thomas S., and Stanley J. MICHAEL. Life Stress and Mental Health. New York: The Free Press, 1963.
The Midtown Manhatten study related to mental health found that one-third of the subjects who showed mental disturbances came from broken homes.

MADOW, Leo, and Sherman E. HARDY. "Incidence and Analysis of the Broken Family in the Background of Neurosis," American Journal of Orthopsychiatry, XVII (July 1947), 521-528.
A review of the case histories of 211 neurotic patients, 76 of whom came from broken families, the remainder from intact families. Some comparisons in background data and present mental illness are made.

MEYER, Marguerite S. The Family without a Father. Denver: Colorado State Department of Public Welfare, 1956, 7 pp. (Reprinted from Rhode Island Welfare, December 1955.)
A brief discussion of the effects on the child when there is no father in the home. The author summarizes many of the problems faced by the mother.

MOUSTAKAS, Clark E. Loneliness. Englewood Cliffs: Prentice-Hall, 1961.
Loneliness is a condition of human life, an experience which enables the individual to sustain, extend, and deepen his humanity.

NEUBAUER, Peter B. "The One-Parent Child and His
Oedipal Development," in Anna Freud, et al., ed.
The Psychoanalytic Study of the Child. New York:
International Universities Press, 1960. Vol. XV,
286-310.
This study shows the effects on children of disturbances
in the oedipal struggle and the variety of oedipal solutions adopted by children with one parent, illustrating
the processes of sexual identification and superego
formation.

OSTROVSKY, Everett S. Children without Men. New
York: Collier Books, 1962.
The case-study material was gathered in a nursery
school setting in which the author was a participant ob-
server. This book details the damaging effect on the
child when the father is absent and stresses the presence
of other male adults in a child's life at all stages.

PARKER, Seymour, and Robert J. KLEINER. "Characteristics of Negro Mothers in Single-Headed Households," Journal of Marriage and the Family, XXVIII
(November 1966), 507-513.
A study of the adjustment and attitudes of negro mothers
in broken and intact homes in order to evaluate the effects of single parenthood on the children. The investigators interviewed 389 intact-family mothers, and 115
single-headed families in Philadelphia.

PASTORAL PSYCHOLOGY. "The Widow, the Divorcée,
and the Single Woman," XVIII (December 1967),
whole issue.
Seven articles discuss the broken family and the social
and religious factors in society related to women who
become "single" again.

POLLACK, Otto. "The Broken Family," in Social Work
and Social Problems, edited by Nathan E. Cohen.
New York: National Association of Social Workers,
1964, pp. 321-339.
The effects of broken families are discussed, and the

approaches of social work to these families are reviewed.

POPENOE, Paul. "Single Parenthood," Family Life,
    XXV (September 1965), 1-3.
Some guidelines for the community in helping the one-
parent mother and her children.

ROSENBERG, Morris. "The Broken Family and the
    Adolescent Self-Image," in Jerold Heiss, ed., Fam-
    ily Roles and Interaction: An Anthology. Chicago:
    Rand McNally, 1958, pp. 516-532.
The author investigates the consequences of various kinds
of broken homes on the adolescent's personality with
special reference to his self-esteem and psychosomatic
illness. The study included 816 broken families. This
article is part of the author's book: Society and the Adolescent Self-Image (Princeton: Princeton University
Press, 1965).

SCANZONI, John. "A Social System Analysis of Dis-
    solved and Existing Marriages," Journal of Mar-
    riage and the Family, XXX (August 1968), 452-461.
The author asks why some groups or social systems remain intact and others do not. His pilot study included
160 intact marriages in an urban area, and 110 dissolved
marriages.

SCHLESINGER, Benjamin. "Parents without Partners,"
    Canadian Welfare, XLII (November 1966), 231-236.
A report of a study of 74 males and females who head
one-parent families in Metropolitan Toronto, completed
at the School of Social Work, University of Toronto.

--------. "The One-Parent Family: An Overview,"
    Family Life Coordinator, XV (October 1966), 133-
    138.
Some statistical presentation of Canadian and American
trends of one-parent families, and a discussion of "Parents Without Partners," the organization for single parents. The different types of one-parent categories are
briefly reviewed.

SMITH, P. M. "Broken Homes and Juvenile Delin-
    quency," Sociology and Social Research, XXXIX
    (May-June 1955), 307-311.
A summary of studies dealing with the relationship of
broken homes to juvenile delinquency.

SPREY, Jetse. "The Study of Single-Parenthood: Some
    Methodological Considerations," The Family Life
    Coordinator, XVI (January-April 1967), 29-34.
The universal characteristics of the single-parent family structure are reviewed and analyzed.

STREAN, Herbert S. "Treatment of Mothers and Sons
    in the Absence of the Father," Social Work, VI
    (July 1961), 29-35.
A preliminary report of a three-year study at a child
guidance clinic in New York. The mothers were all one-
parent family heads.

STRINGER, Elizabeth A. "Homemaker Service to the
    Single-Parent Family," Social Casework, XLVIII
    (February 1967), 75-80.
A discussion of homemaker service to 27 single-parent
families in New York, with case illustrations. The
practical use of the homemaker service for this type of
family is demonstrated.

TANNER, Virginia L. Selected Social Work Concepts
    for Public Welfare Workers. Washington, D. C.:
    Bureau of Family Services, Welfare Administration,
    1964.
Chapters VIII to X of this book contain material on the
concepts of the one-parent family. Teaching cases are
included as illustrative material.

THOMAS, Margaret Mary. "Children with Absent
    Fathers," Journal of Marriage and the Family,
    XXX (February 1968), 189-196.
Forty-seven 9 to 11 year old children of low socio-
economic background from father-absent homes were
compared with a matched control group with fathers

present in the home.

THORMAN, George. Broken Homes. New York: Public
    Affairs Committee, 1958. Pamphlet #135.
A digest of material related to families which are broken
by death, desertion, separation, and divorce.

TOBY, Jackson. "The Differential Impact of Family
    Disorganization," American Sociological Review,
    XXII (October 1957), 505-512.
An examination of the hypothesis that the incidence of
broken homes is greater among families of delinquents
than among families generally.

WALLENSTEIN, N. Character and Personality of Chil-
    dren from Broken Homes. New York: Teachers
    College, Columbia University Mono. No. 721, 1937.
The experimental group in this study consisted of 400
boys and girls from broken homes and the control group
included 1,600 boys and girls from normal homes.

WATTENBERG, Ben J., and Richard M. SCAMMON.
    This U.S.A.: An Unexpected Family Portrait of
    194,067,296 Americans Drawn from the Census.
    Garden City: Doubleday, 1965.
Includes material on one-parent families. The Appendix
has a compendium of the most useful 1960 Census facts
related to the American family.

WOLF, Anna, and Lucille STEIN. The One-Parent
    Family. New York: Public Affairs Committee and
    the Child Study Association of America, 1959.
This pamphlet, directed to single parents, gives advice
on problems arising from death, divorce, separation,
and desertion of one parent—mother as well as father.
Emphasis is on what to tell children and on practical
handling of emotional reactions.

WOOD, Margaret Mary. Paths of Loneliness. New
    York: Columbia University Press, 1953.
An examination of lonely people and their social and

psychological reactions.

WYLIE, Howard E., and Ralph A. DEGADO. "A Pattern of Mother-Son Relationship Involving the Absence of the Father," American Journal of Orthopsychiatry, XXIX (July 1959), 644-649.
Nearly all 20 cases of boys whose fathers were absent, studied at the Worcester Youth Guidance Center, showed learning problems and difficulties in handling their aggressive impulses.

WYNN, Margaret. Fatherless Children. London: Michael Joseph, 1964.
An examination of the one-parent family in England. The author discusses social and legal rights and social services for these families. The appendix includes statistical tables on fatherless families in England.

ZUKERMAN, Jacob T. "Family Disorganization," in Encyclopedia of Social Work, edited by Harry L. Lurie. New York: National Association of Social Workers, 1965, pp. 305-309.
A short statistical review of family breakdown in the United States, with some of the community resources available for families who break down.

## DESERTION AND SEPARATION

BACH, G. R. "Father Fantasies and Father Typing in Father-separated Children," Child Development, XVII (March 1946), 63-80.
Twenty 6 to 10 year old boys and girls were observed at doll play. Their fathers had been absent because of the war for one to three year periods. A matched father-present control group was also used.

CANADIAN WELFARE COUNCIL. Family Desertion. Ottawa, 1961.

The causes and effects of desertion are summarized, and recommendations are made to improve community resources in order to reduce the number.

--------. Papers on Desertion: 1955. Ottawa, 1956. Three papers discuss the concern about desertions, the implications for family life, and the family court and desertions.

CRAIN, Alan J., and Caroline S. STAMON. "Intermittent Absence of Fathers and Children's Perception of Parents," Journal of Marriage and the Family, XXVII (August 1965), 344-347. Two classes of second graders, of whom 30 of the fathers were Navy personnel and absent intermittently, were given a two-test battery to determine their perception of their fathers.

GARDNER, G. E. "Separation of the Parents and the Emotional Life of the Child," Mental Hygiene, XL (January 1956), 53-64. The effect of parental absence on the child's concept of self and of other human beings.

HARPER, Fowler V., and Jerome H. SKOLNICK. Problems of the Family. Revised edition. New York: Bobbs-Merrill, 1963. A legal-social science approach to family problems including separation and divorce (Chapters IV, VI, and VII).

HILL, Reuben. Families under Stress. New York: Harper and Bros., 1949. A study of 135 families in 1947 in Iowa of all socio-economic groups. The majority had married during the Depression years, and at the time of the study the fathers had been drafted into military service.

HOLT, Herbert, and Charles WINICK. "Some Psychodynamics in Divorce and Separation." See annotation under DIVORCE.

HUNT, Morton M.  The World of the Formerly Married.
    New York: McGraw-Hill, 1966.
A journalist examines American patterns of separated
and divorced men and women.  The effect on adults and
children is vividly demonstrated by case illustrations.

KUNDERT, Elizabeth.  "Fear of Desertion by Mother,"
    American Journal of Orthopsychiatry, XVII (April
    1947), 326-336.
A study using case materials from a mental health clinic
to indicate the fears of children about possible desertion
by their mothers.

LEICHTY, Mary M.  "The Effect of Father-Absence
    during Early Childhood upon the Oedipal Situation
    as Reflected in Young Adults," Merrill-Palmer
    Quarterly, VI (July 1960), 212-217.
Thirty-three male students at college whose fathers
were overseas during World War II while the subjects
were between the ages of 3 and 5 were studied.  A control group was also used.  The findings indicate that the
absence of father during the oedipal period affected some
aspects of personality development.

LERNER, Samuel H.  "Effects of Desertion on Family
    Life," Social Casework, XXXV (January 1954), 3-8.
This article, written by a psychiatrist, discusses the
direct and indirect effects on the children of desertion
by a father.  The effect of the desertion will depend on
the degree of emancipation, or the amount of dependence-
independence, that the children have achieved.  This, of
course, depends on their stage of development and their
emotional security.

MacINTOSH, Houston.  "Separation Problems in Military
    Wives," American Journal of Psychiatry, CXXV
    (August 1968), 156-161.
Sixty-three wives of military servicemen separated from
their families were compared with 113 wives not separated but needing psychiatric help.  The psychodynamics
of separation are discussed.

MONAHAN, Thomas P. , and William M. KEPHART.
"Divorce and Desertion by Religious and Mixed-
Religious Groups." See annotation under DIVORCE.

MORRIS, Pauline. Prisoners and Their Families. New
York: Hart, 1965.
A study in England of a random sample of 837 prisoners.
The men were interviewed in prison and their wives at
home. The adjustment of the families is discussed at
length.

NEILL, Frances E. , and Ralph J. GLOVER. "Report
of a Study of One Hundred Cases of Desertion,"
The Family, IX (January 1929), 287-291.
Fourteen women and 86 men who deserted their families
were studied. The findings are summarized.

OGBURN, W. F. "Marital Separation, " American
Journal of Sociology, XLIX (1944), 316-323.
Permanent separation in modern urban society may begin without intention of permanency. For example, a
man working away from home, intending to return to or
to send for the family, drifts unintentionally toward
permanent separation because of communication problems.

ONTARIO LAW REFORM COMMISSION. Family Law
Project. See annotation under DIVORCE.

REIMER, M. D. "The Effect on Character Development of Prolonged or Frequent Absence of Parents, "
Mental Hygiene, XXXIII (April 1949), 293-297.
The relation of parental deprivation due to various
causes and psychoneuroses in patients is discussed in
a psychoanalytic framework.

STEIGMAN, Joseph E. "The Deserted Family, " Social
Casework, XXXVIII (April 1957), 167-171.
The author estimates that five-and-one-half million
women and children in the U.S.A. lack adequate support
because of desertion. He also estimates that there are

one million men involved who have deserted, with an
additional 100,000 men deserting each year. He discusses some of the services that are required by the
deserted family, including practical aid, counseling,
and legal advice.

ZUKERMAN, Jacob T. "Some Jewish Aspects of Fam-
    ily Desertion," in Jacob Freid, ed., Judaism and
    the Community. New York: Thomas Joseloff, 1968,
    pp. 45-52.
A report of the National Desertion Bureau, and some of
the types of cases handled by them.

--------. "A Socio-Legal Approach to Family Deser-
    tion," Marriage and Family Living, VIII (August
    1950), 83-84.
Desertion is a method employed to break up the marriage
relationship for hundreds of thousands of unhappy couples
who cannot afford to pay for divorce actions. This article contains some important statistical findings.


DIVORCE


BERGLER, Edmund. Divorce Won't Help. New York:
    Hart, 1948.
A psychoanalyst shows that divorce will not alleviate or
cure marriage problems, unless the neurotic elements
which broke up the first marriage are eliminated.

BERNARD, Jessie. "The Adjustments of Married
    Mates," in Handbook of Marriage and the Family,
    edited by Harold T. Christensen. Chicago: Rand
    McNally, 1964, pp. 675-739.
Divorce as outcome of failure of marital adjustment is
included in this paper.

BERNSTEIN, Norman R. "Problems of Children with
    Divorced Parents," Feelings, VI (April 1964), 1-4.
Some guidance to divorced mothers in relation to their

children. Three case histories illustrate the presentation.

BRAILEY, F. W. L. Why Divorce? Toronto: United
    Church of Canada, 1953.
This pamphlet discusses divorce in Canada and outlines
some of the Christian theological viewpoints related to
divorce.

BURCHINAL, L. G. "Characteristics of Adolescents
    from Unbroken, Broken and Reconstituted Families,"
    Journal of Marriage and the Family, XXVI (February
    1964), 44-51.
The relationship of divorce and remarriage of parents to
developmental characteristics of children is observed in
a sample of 1,566 children in the 7th and 8th grades in
Cedar Rapids, Iowa.

CANADA. Senate and House of Commons. Report on
    Divorce. Ottawa: Queen's Printer, 1967.
The final report of a joint committee of the Senate and
House of Commons to recommend revised legislation in
relation to divorce in Canada. The suggestions of the
committee were adopted, and put into law July 1, 1968.

CANTOR, Donald J. "The Right of Divorce," The Single
    Parent, X (June 1967), 4-7.
An attorney attacks the existing divorce procedures and
makes suggestions for reform, especially in child-
custody cases.

CARTER, Hugh, and Alexander PLATERIS. "Trends in
    Divorce and Family Disruption," Health, Education,
    and Welfare Indicators (September 1963), pp. 5-14.
A statistical analysis of divorce trends and separation
among families in the United States, 1920-1960.

DAVIDSON, Bill. "Help Me, I'm Alone," The Single
    Parent, IX (November 1966), 4-6.
The program called SOS is organized so that people
caught in the turmoil of divorce gather together to help
each other fight despair and loneliness.

DAY, Lincoln H. "Patterns of Divorce in Australia and
the United States," American Sociological Review,
XXIX (August 1964), 504-522.
Australians resort less to divorce than Americans, and
generally only after a much longer duration of marriage.
The reasons for this difference are discussed.

DESPERT, J. Louise. Children of Divorce. Garden
City: Doubleday, Dolphin paperback, 1962.
This book, the author states, is an attempt "to sketch
the whole experience of marriage failure in its impact
on the child." The author discusses the importance of
"emotional divorce," a situation which always precedes
legal divorce, although it is not always followed by it.

EMERSON, James G. Divorce, The Church, and Remarriage. Philadelphia: The Westminster Press,
1961.
"The remarriage laws of the churches are neither
Christian nor humanitarian; but emotional and dictator-
ial."

FAMILY LIFE. "Statistics of Divorce," XXV (April
1965), 1-3.
A summary of the divorce rates in 48 states in order of
frequency of divorce, taken from the 1960 Vital Statistics.

GENDELL, Murray, and Hans L. ZETTERBERG. A
Sociological Almanac for the United States. New
York: Charles Scribner's Sons, 1964.
Contains statistical data on family life, including mar-
riage and divorce up to 1960.

GOLDMAN, Ralph C. "He's Still Their Father," The
Single Parent, VIII (June 1965), 5-7 and 33.
An attorney spells out the obligations and rights of each
parent in divorce actions.

GOODE, William J. After Divorce. Glencoe: The Free
Press, 1956.
A discussion of the implications for divorce and remar-
riage, based on the author's research in Detroit.

--------. "Problems in Postdivorce Adjustment,"
  American Sociological Review, XIV (June 1949),
  394-401.
A pilot study of the postdivorce adjustment of 100 urban
mothers.

HARPER, Fowler V., and Jerome H. SKOLNICK. Problems of the Family. See annotation under GENERAL.

HOLT, Herbert, and Charles WINICK. "Some Psychodynamics in Divorce and Separation," Mental Hygiene, XLIX (July 1965), 443-452.
Three cases are presented at length, and the authors discuss treatment related to the termination of a marriage
and the effects on the spouses. The orientation is psychoanalytic.

HUNT, Morton M. "Wanted Divorce Counselors," The
  Single Parent, X (February-March 1967), 4-8.
Divorced people should be aided rather than impeded in
their efforts to make the break and live successfully in
the postmarital world.

--------. The World of the Formerly Married. See
  annotation under DESERTION AND SEPARATION.

ILGENFRITZ, Marjorie P. "Mothers on Their Own."
  See annotation under GENERAL.

JACOBSON, Paul H. American Marriage and Divorce.
  New York: Rinehart, 1959.
Comprehensive data on marriages by age differentials,
marital status, and race.

KAPIT, Hanna. "The Widowed and the Divorced." See
  annotation under WIDOWHOOD.

KEPHART, William M. "Legal and Procedural Aspects
  of Marriage and Divorce," in Handbook of Marriage
  and the Family, edited by Harold T. Christensen.
  Chicago: Rand McNally, 1964, pp. 944-968.

The socio-legal aspects of divorce, grounds for divorce, annulments, legal separation, and research implications related to divorce are discussed.

--------. "The Duration of Marriage," American Sociological Review, XIX (June 1954), 287-295.
It is desirable to know not only what proportion of marriages are terminating in divorce, but also how long these marriages have lasted (duration). Statistical data for Philadelphia County for 1937-1950 are examined.

LANDIS, Judson T. "Social Correlates of Divorce and Non-divorce among the Unhappy Married," Marriage and Family Living, XXV (May 1963), 178-180.
Those who marry at very young ages and who find themselves in an unhappy marriage tend to get out of their marriage through divorce.

LASCH, Christopher. "Divorce and the Family in America," The Single Parent, X (April 1967), 4-9.
A historian looks at the changing attitudes of marriage and divorce in our society.

LAW AND CONTEMPORARY PROBLEMS. "Divorce: A Re-examination of Basic Concepts," XVIII (Winter 1953), whole issue.
Nine papers look at divorce, separation, annulments, and the divorce court.

--------. "Children of Divorced Parents," X (Summer 1944), whole issue.
Eleven papers discuss the sociological, legal, and psychiatric aspects related to children of divorced parents.

LEVINGER, George. "Marital Cohesiveness and Dissolution: An Integrative Review," Journal of Marriage and the Family, XXVII (February 1965), 19-28.
Findings from major investigations of marriage and divorce are used to develop an elementary framework for integrating the determinants of marriage durability and divorce.

LITWAK, Eugene. "Divorce Law as a Means of Social
    Control," in Edwin T. Thomas ed., Behavioural
    Science for Social Workers. New York: The Free
    Press, 1967, pp. 178-187.
A discussion of the divorce law as punishment, therapy,
and education.

LOCKE, Harvey J. "Predicting Marital Adjustment by
    Comparing a Divorced and a Happily Married Group,"
    American Sociological Review, XII (April 1947), 187-
    191.
This study involved 925 native-born Protestants (201 divorced couples, 123 individual divorcées, and a control
group of 200 married couples) of native-born parents,
a group claimed to constitute a fairly representative
sample of the population.

MACE, David R. "Marriage Breakdown or Matrimonial
    Offense: A Clinical or Legal Approach to Divorce,"
    The American University Law Review, XIV (June
    1965), 178-188.
The diversity and complexity of laws and practices in the
United States are examined briefly, and better approaches
to divorce are presented.

McDERMOTT, John F. "Parental Divorce in Early
    Childhood," American Journal of Psychiatry, CXXIV
    (April 1968), 1424-1432.
The legal event of parental divorce presents acute problems to the very young child, since it involves an abrupt
change in his daily life. A sample of 10 children of nursery school age is examined.

MONAHAN, Thomas P. "When Married Couples Part:
    Statistical Trends and Relationships in Divorce,"
    American Sociological Review, XXVII (October
    1962), 625-633.
Through examination of data, it is shown that "the oft-
repeated sociological reference to the 3rd or 4th years
of marriage as showing the highest percentage of divorce decrees . . . and the implication given thereby

that marriage crises grow until then, is a spurious statistical fact." Some studies have failed to take into account the fact that the divorce decree usually arrives some years after the actual family breakup.

--------. "The Duration of Marriage to Divorce: Second Marriages and Migratory Types," Marriage and Family Living, XXI (May 1959), 134-138.
With each successive divorce experience the probability of divorce increases and the speed of dissolution also rises. A statistical analysis in Iowa, 1953.

--------. "The Changing Probability of Divorce," American Sociological Review, V (August 1940), 536-545.
What are the chances that a marriage will be terminated by a divorce? Divorce data in America from 1892 to 1932 are analyzed.

MONAHAN, Thomas P., and William M. KEPHART. "Divorce and Desertion by Religious and Mixed-Religious Groups," American Journal of Sociology, LIX (March 1954), 454-465.
A statistical analysis of divorce and desertion as found in the three major religious groups of Catholics, Jews, and Protestants.

MUDD, Emily H. "The Social Worker's Function in Divorce Proceedings," Law and Contemporary Problems, XVIII (Winter 1953), 66-71.
A skillful caseworker with special training and experience in marriage and family counseling can enlist the cooperation of a couple who do not want counseling but who have been requested by authority to seek it. The dilemma of whether the caseworker can or should make a contribution in such a situation is apparently solved by assuming that the divorce applicants are too immature and unrealistic to seek help voluntarily.

O'HARA, Ralph C. The Divorcée. Derby, Connecticut: Monarch Books, 1962.

Seven case histories by a doctor illustrate the emotional problems faced by women who have shed their husbands through a divorce.

O'NEILL, William L.  Divorce in the Progressive Era. New Haven: Yale University Press, 1967.
The author focuses on the 1880-1920 period to examine the battle between conservatives and liberals in relation to divorce reform.

ONTARIO LAW REFORM COMMISSION.  Family Law Project.  Toronto: Parliament Buildings, 1968.
A series of working papers related to marriage, divorce, and separation have been published by the family law project.  The papers examine existing legislation in Ontario, and include statistical data related to family breakdown.

PAGET, Norman W.  Counseling Services to Parents and Children Involved in Divorce Proceedings.  San Bernardino: California State Department of Social Welfare, July 1960.
This is a report on a demonstration project to determine the need for assertive casework techniques and for counseling with persons who file for divorce.

PANNOR, Harry, and Sylvia SCHILD.  "Impact of Divorce on Children," Child Welfare, XXXIX (February 1960), 6-10.
Using examples from the Jewish Big Brother Association of Los Angeles, the author discusses parent-child relationships at the time of divorce.

PEEKE, Jessie E.  "Counseling Parents in Divorce," in Fred DelliQuadri, ed., Helping the Family in Urban Society.  New York: Columbia University Press, 1963, pp. 119-132.
Eighty-nine parents contemplating divorce and 53 separated couples in San Bernardino County, California, were part of a special project of counseling services offered to families.  The author summarizes the results of the project.

94

PEELE, Catherine Groves. "Social and Psychological Effects of the Availability and Granting of Alimony on the Spouses," Law and Contemporary Problems, VI (Spring 1939), 283-292.
The prevailing attitudes in a person's social matrix may influence his attitude about paying alimony, e.g., to an able-bodied young woman without young children, or to the guilty party in the divorce proceedings. In most cases, legal pressure only tends to aggravate the existing feelings between the spouses.

PINARD, Maurice. "Marriage and Divorce Decisions and the Larger Social System: A Case Study in Social Change," Social Forces, XLIV (March 1966), 341-353.
Marriage and divorce decisions have become increasingly affected by common causes located outside the social world of the family system, and are now dependent on those of the larger social system.

PLANT, James S. "The Psychiatrist Views Children of Divorced Parents," Law and Contemporary Problems, X (Summer 1944), 807-818.
The child tends to be forgotten in the adult struggle: one or another child is rejected as being identified with the rejected partner, or the child becomes a pawn in the game. Disposition of the children should be based on "where they have their best chance for security."

POSPISHIL, Victor J. Divorce and Remarriage: Towards a New Catholic Teaching. New York: Herder and Herder, 1967.
A detailed argument by an American canon lawyer for permitting remarriage of divorcees in the Catholic Church. The author is an Eastern Orthodox theology professor.

ROHNER, Louise. The Divorcée's Handbook. Garden City: Doubleday, 1967.
A self-help book for the divorced woman. The advice by the author, who has herself experienced a divorce, is

practical and attempts to help the divorced woman adjust
to her new status.

RUTLEDGE, Aaron L. "Should the Marriage Counselor
      Ever Recommend Divorce," Marriage and Family
      Living, XXV (August 1963), 319-325.
Divorce is not the best solution to most of the personality
and relationship problems seen in marriage counseling.

SCHWARTZ, Anne C. "Reflections on Divorce and Re-
      marriage," Social Casework, XLIX (April 1968),
      213-217.
A commentary on the changing attitudes towards divorce,
and some views on the new roles and new adjustments in
second marriages.

STEWART, Charles W. "Counseling the Divorcee,"
      Pastoral Psychology, XIV (January 1963), 10-16.
Pastoral marriage counseling helps the individual to
understand what has happened to him once the marriage
fails.

STOUFFER, Samuel A., and Lyle M. SPENCER. "Mar-
      riage and Divorce in Recent Years," The Annals,
      CLXXXVIII (November 1936), 56-69.
A statistical paper which outlines the trends of marriage
and divorce in the Depression period in the United States.

UNITED CHURCH OF CANADA. Marriage Breakdown,
      Divorce and Remarriage. Toronto, 1962.
The report of the Commission on Christian Marriage
and Divorce looks at Canadian trends in relation to divorce, remarriage, and family disorganization. Recommendations are made for tackling these social
problems.

UNIVERSITY OF CHICAGO, LAW SCHOOL. Conference
      on Divorce. Chicago, February 1952.
Ten contributors examine divorce practice, therapeutic
aspects of divorce, and family conflicts around divorce.

VINCENT, Clark E. "Divorced and Married 'Unwed'
    Mothers," Sexology, XXVIII (May 1962), 674-679.
A discussion of the illicit pregnancies of divorced and
married women.

WALLER, Willard. The Old Love and the New.
    Carbondale: Southern Illinois University Press,
    1958.
This is a new edition of a volume originally published in
1930. It contains a new introduction by Bernard Farber.
The book focuses on the social-psychological consequences of divorce.

WALLER, Willard, and Reuben HILL. "The Processes
    of Alienation," in Jerold Heiss, ed., Family Roles
    and Interaction: An Anthology. Chicago: Rand
    McNally, 1968, pp. 483-500.
A couple divorces after their conflict leads to a number
of changes which make divorce seem an appropriate and
acceptable solution.


WIDOWHOOD


BARTLETT, Claude J., and John E. HORROCKS. "A
    Study of the Needs Status of Adolescents from Broken
    Homes," Journal of Genetic Psychology, XCIII
    (September 1958), 153-159.
Questionnaires were given to 44 youths from homes
broken by death of one parent, and to a control group of
44 youths from unbroken families. The adolescents
from broken homes tended to seek affection in attention
from the opposite sex and needed more of it.

BECK, Frances. Diary of a Widow. Boston: Beacon
    Press, 1965.
A diary kept by a woman with three children, who was
widowed at age 35.

BECKER, H. "The Sorrow of Bereavement," Journal
    of Abnormal and Social Psychology, XXVII (October-

December 1933), 391-410.
A summary of hypotheses concerned with the social psychology of bereavement from case histories and literary samples.

BERARDO, Felix M. "Widowhood Status in the United States: Perspective on a Neglected Aspect of the Family Life Cycle," The Family Coordinator, XVII (July 1968), 191-203.
An examination of selected socio-demographic conditions which characterize contemporary widowhood status reveals a dismal picture. The literature on widowhood is also reviewed.

--------. Social Adaptation to Widowhood among a Rural Urban Aged Population. Pullman: Washington State University, College of Agriculture, Bulletin #689, December 1967.
A report of a study of 44 widowers and 181 widows, whose medium duration of widowhood was 10.8 years for females, and for males 11.8 years. All of the subjects were over the age of 65, and lived in Thurston County, Washington.

CHAMPAGNE, Marion. Facing Life Alone. New York: Bobbs-Merrill, 1964.
A widowed lawyer with two children discusses the feelings of widowhood, and how to move ahead to a new family life.

CLAYTON, Paula, Lynn DESMARAIS, and George WINOKUR. "A Study of Normal Bereavement," American Journal of Psychiatry, CXXV (August 1968), 168-178.
The symptoms of bereavement were studied with 40 subjects. Depressed mood, sleep disturbance, and crying occurred with more than half.

ELIOT, Thomas D. "Bereavement: Inevitable But Not Insurmountable," in Howard Becker, and Reuben Hill, eds., Family Marriage and Parenthood.

Boston: C. C. Heath, 1948, pp. 641-668.
A full discussion of bereavement, including a review of existing socio-psychological literature from 1927 to 1946.


--------. "The Bereaved Family," The Annals, CLX
    (March 1932), 184-190.
An attempt to classify ways in which family members respond to family bereavement and the subsequent effects upon the whole family.


--------. "Bereavement as a Problem for Family Re-
    search and Technique," The Family, XI (June 1930),
    114-116.
A research guide to study bereavement in socio-psychological terms.

GLASER, Barney G. , and Anselm L. STRAUSS. Aware-
    ness of Dying. Chicago: Aldine, 1965.
Two sociologists examine the dying patient in hospital, and his family. Death as a social ritual is fully discussed.


GOODE, William J. World Revolution and Family Pat-
    terns. New York: The Free Press, 1963.
The author deals with the status of widowhood in various world cultures (see Index, p. 431).


GORER, Geoffrey. Death, Grief and Mourning: A Study
    of Contemporary Society. Garden City: Doubleday,
    1965.
A 1963 study in Great Britain of the social denial and the individual repudiation of mourning. The sample included 1, 628 people of both sexes over the age of 16, of every social class, and coming from every region in Great Britain.


ILGENFRITZ, Marjorie P. "Mothers on Their Own."
    See annotation under GENERAL.

ISAACS, Susan. "Fatherless Children," Childhood and
     After. London: Routledge and Kegan Paul, 1948,
     Chap. 12.
This chapter, originally a paper written in 1945 about
children who lost fathers in the war, is based on clinical experience. The orientation is psychoanalytic. The
younger the child when the father dies, the worse the
psychological effects, even in the first year of life, since
"too young to understand" does not mean "too young to
feel." A section on handling in the school is also included.

JACKSON, Edgar N. Understanding Grief. New York:
     Abingdon Press, 1957.
A Methodist minister who has also studied psychotherapy
has written this integrated study of the psychological,
theological, and philosophical dimensions of bereavement.

KAPIT, Hanna. "The Widowed and the Divorced," The
     Single Parent, VIII (June 1965), 8-9 and 37.
A psychoanalyst examines the problems which face the
widowed and the divorced.

KEPHART, W. M. "Status after Death," American
     Sociological Review, XV (October 1950), 635-643.
The funeral, burial, and bereavement practices among
the social classes in the urban setting of Philadelphia.

KLEIN, Melanie. "Mourning and Its Relation to Manic-
     Depressive States," in Contributions to Psycho-
     Analysis. London: Hogarth Press, 1948, pp. 311-
     338.
Mourning is described as inevitably a psychological illness, from which recovery must be made in very specific ways. The difference between normal mourning
("normal" but still an illness) and abnormal mourning,
the negative outcomes possible for people who do not
experience mourning, and the possibility of significant
enriching of some people at a certain time of mourning
are discussed.

LANGER, Marion. Learning To Live as a Widow. New
York: Julian Messner, 1957.
A discussion of bereavement and the feelings involved.
Also covers the areas of finances, careers, social life,
effect on children and adolescents, adjustment to dating,
and remarriage.

LINDEMANN, Erich. "Acute Grief: Symptoms and
Management, " American Journal of Psychiatry, CI
(September 1944), 141-148.
Studies of reaction to situations of death of a member of
a family are documented by case histories, and methods
for dealing with these reactions are suggested.

LUCAS, Rex A. "Social Implications of the Immediacy
of Death, " The Canadian Review of Sociology and
Anthropology, V (February 1968), 1-16.
"Death is an experience faced but once by each individual; yet dying, like living, is a social role, and it is in
this sense that death is considered here." A full bibliography related to this topic is included in this article.

MARRIS, Peter. Widows and Their Families. London:
Routledge and Kegan Paul, 1958.
An Institute of Community Studies survey of 72 widows
in the East End of London, England, whose husbands
died in youth or middle age.

McGEACHY, D. P. A Matter of Life and Death.
Richmond: John Knox Press, 1966.
A Presbyterian minister offers some guidance to those
who have been bereaved.

METROPOLITAN LIFE INSURANCE CO. "The American
Widow, " Statistical Bulletin, XXXII (November 1962),
1-7.
Gives some interesting statistics of widowhood in the
United States, which increases by more than 100, 000 a
year today compared with 80, 000 in the 1920s and 50, 000
at the turn of the century. Widows currently outnumber
widowers four to one compared with two to one about 50

years ago. About 10 percent of all women between the
ages of 45 to 54 are widows.

MITCHELL, Nellie L. "The Significance of the Loss of
    Father through Death," American Journal of Ortho-
    psychiatry, XXIV (March 1964), 279-280.
A digest of a paper delivered at the annual meeting of the
American Orthopsychiatric Association. The author reports on 5 case histories and discusses the psychological
implications of the death of father to these families.

OSBORNE, Ernest. When You Lose a Loved One. New
    York: Public Affairs Committee, 1958. Pamphlet
    #269.
A short guide to the family who is faced with the death of
one of the family members.

PENISTON, Hugh D. "The Importance of 'Death Educa-
    tion' in Family Life," Family Life Coordinator, XI
    (January 1962), 15-18.
A plea to include the topic of death and its implications
in courses on family life education.

PSYCHIATRIC OPINION. "Death and Responsibility,"
    III (August 1966), whole issue.
Three papers discuss the death of a member of a family
from the religious, social, psychological, and psychiatric points of view.

RICH, Louise Dickinson. Only Parent. Philadelphia:
    J. B. Lippincott, 1953.
In this book about the life of a single widowed parent
and her children, the author shows that life as a single
parent need not be a disastrous affair for the individual
or her children.

ROSEN, Roslyn. "The Other Side of Loneliness," The
    Single Parent, VIII (December 1965), 4-5 and 34.
A widow's poignant personal story, especially in relation
to grief and mourning.

SHUDDE, Louis O., and Lenore A. EPSTEIN. "Or-
    phaned: A Diminishing Problem," Social Security
    Bulletin, XVIII (March 1955), 17-19.
A statistical analysis of orphanhood in America, 1920-
1954.

SIGGINS, Lorraine D. "Mourning: A Critical Survey of
    the Literature," The International Journal of Psycho-
    Analysis, XLVII (Part I. 1966), 14-25.
This paper describes the psycho-analytic model related
to the death of a loved person. Both normal and path-
ological mourning are discussed and the variety of reactions to death are summarized.

SPIEGELMAN, Mortimer. "The Broken Family: Widow-
    hood and Orphanhood," The Annals, CLXXXVIII
    (November 1936), 117-130.
A statistical analysis of the 1930 Census in the United
States in relation to widows, widowers, and orphans.

STATISTICAL BULLETIN. "Death in the Family,"
    XLVIII (April 1967), 5-7.
A statistical analysis of chances for survival in America.
Chances of death in families are presented in tabular
form.

ULRICH, Joan. "Life without Father," The Single
    Parent, IX (January 1966), 4-6 and 33.
A widow who has been a one-parent mother for 10 years
discusses her active life.

VINCENT, Clark E. "The Loss of Parents and Psycho-
    somatic Illness," Sociology and Social Research,
    XXXIX (July-August 1955), 404-408.
Based on a study of 34 male and 20 female patients re-
ferred to a psychiatric clinic, this paper discusses the
relation of psychosomatic ailments to loss of parent.

WARGOTZ, Helen. "The Adjustment of Children in
    Motherless Homes," The Single Parent, XI (May-
    June 1968), 4-10.

This is a report of a study of 22 widowed fathers, with incomes ranging from $7,000 to $50,000 per annum. There were 46 children involved (21 girls, 25 boys) ranging in age from 2 to 21 years at the time of their mother's death. The problems faced by the fathers are discussed.

WOLF, Anna W. M. Helping Your Child to Understand Death. New York: Child Study Association of America, 1958.
This pamphlet aims to help parents deal with children's general questions about death, and children's experience of the death of parents, siblings, pets, relatives, and friends.


# THE UNMARRIED PARENT


BERNSTEIN, Rose. "Unmarried Parents and Their Families," Child Welfare, XLV (April 1966), 185-193.
An attempt to answer the question, "What do we know about unmarried fathers?" The role of the father is discussed and suggestions for service to him are made.

BOWERMAN, Charles E., Donald P. IRISH, and Hallowell POPE. Unwed Motherhood: Personal and Social Consequences. Chapel Hill: Institute for Research in Social Science, 1966.
This study includes the findings of four separate studies, three of which included 1,630 white and negro unmarried mothers, and one is a demographic study of illegitimacy in North Carolina, 1948-1960.

CHASKEL, Ruth. "The Unmarried Mother: Is She Different?," Child Welfare, XLVI (February 1967), 65-75.
The thesis of this paper is that the unmarried mother constitutes a cross section of the female population.

Some comments on the unmarried father are included.

CHILDREN. "Unmarried Parents: What Is and Is Not
    Being Done for Them and about Them," X (March-
    April 1963), whole issue.
Six papers discuss illegitimacy, services for the unmarried mother, prevention of illegitimacy, and the unmarried father.

DYMES, Bohumil. "A Brief History of Illegitimacy,"
    Canada's Health and Welfare, XX (December 1965),
    2-3.
A brief historical account of illegitimacy from Roman
times to the present English Elizabethan laws.

FALK, Ursula A., and Gerhard J. FALK. "The Un-
    married Mother: A Sociological Profile," Family
    Life Coordinator, XIV (January 1965), 17-19.
The sociological background of the unmarried mother is
analyzed. About 6 percent of babies born in the United
States are born out of wedlock.

FUTTERMAN, Samuel, and Jean LIVERMORE. "Pu-
    tative Fathers," Journal of Social Casework,
    XXVIII (May 1947), 174-178.
The "double standard" related to out-of-wedlock pregnancy is discussed, with case illustrations of unmarried
fathers.

HERZOG, Elizabeth. "Some Notes about Unmarried
    Fathers," Child Welfare, XLV (April 1966), 194-
    197.
Some of the misconceptions about unmarried fathers are
cleared up by the author.

--------. "The Chronic Revolution: Births out of Wed-
    lock," Clinical Pediatrics, V (February 1966), 130-
    135.
The crisis view of non-wedlock births promotes punitive
attitudes in society. Statistical data related to births in
1963 illustrate the paper.

MARSH, Marguerite. "Common Attitudes toward the
  Unmarried Father," in National Conference of So-
  cial Work Proceedings, 1940. New York: Columbia
  University Press, 1940, pp. 377-388.
An examination of the attitudes of society and social
agencies toward the unmarried father.

MEYER, Henry J., Edgar F. BORGATTA, and David
  FANSHEL. "Unwed Mothers' Decisions about Their
  Babies: An Interim Replication Study," Child Wel-
  fare, XXXVIII (February 1959), 1-6.
A study of 59 unwed mothers (38 white, 21 negro) of
whom three-fifths retained custody of their babies.

MEYER, Henry J., Wyatt JONES, and Edgar F.
  BORGOTTA. "The Decision by Unmarried Mothers
  to Keep Their Babies," Social Work, I (April 1956),
  103-109.
A report of a study of 60 unmarried mothers (20 white
and 40 negro) who decided to keep their babies.

MONAHAN, Thomas P. "Premarital Pregnancy in the
  United States: A Critical Review and Some New
  Findings," Eugenics Quarterly, VII (September
  1960), 133-147.
A review of 56 studies of premarital pregnancy, and
commentary on existing trends in America up to 1960.

PANNOR, Reuben, and Byron W. EVANS. "The Unmarried Father: An Integral Part of Casework Services to the Unmarried Mother," Child Welfare,
  XLVI (March 1967), 150-155.
The approach to the unmarried mother must include
services to the unmarried father, who has many of the
same problems.

PANNOR, Reuben, Fred MASSARIK, and Byron W.
  EVANS. The Unmarried Father. Los Angeles:
  Vista Del Mar Child Care Service, 1967.
A report of methods, findings, and implications for so-
cial work practice of a study of 94 unmarried fathers

and 222 unmarried mothers in California.

PERLMAN, Helen Harris. "Unmarried Mothers," in
    Social Work and Social Problems, edited by Nathan
    E. Cohen. New York: National Association of So-
    cial Workers, 1964, pp. 270-320.
An examination of the unmarried mother as a social
problem in America. The social work profession in this
area is analyzed and reviewed.

POPE, Hallowell. "Unmarried Mothers and Their Sex
    Partners," Journal of Marriage and the Family,
    XXIX (August 1967), 555-567.
A study of 387 white and 552 negro women in selected
North Carolina counties in 1960-61 who had their first
child out of wedlock. The characteristics and relationships of their sex partners are examined.

REED, Ellery. "Unmarried Mothers Who Kept Their
    Babies," Children, XII (May-June 1965), 118-119.
A short summary of a study of 118 unmarried mothers
in Cincinnati, Ohio, who kept their babies.

REED, Ellery, and Ruth LATIMER. A Study of Un-
    married Mothers Who Kept Their Babies.
    Cincinnati: Social Welfare Research Inc., 1963.
A study of 118 unmarried mothers who kept their babies
(127 children). The sample included white and negro
women known to welfare and health departments in the
Cincinnati area.

REIDER, Norman. "The Unmarried Father," American
    Journal of Orthopsychiatry, XVIII (April 1948), 230-
    237.
The psychological effects of the pregnancy on unmarried
fathers is analyzed. The various types and categories
of unmarried fathers are examined.

REINER, Beatrice Simcox. "The Real World of the
    Teen-age Negro Mother," Child Welfare, XLVII
    (July 1968), 391-396.

Unwed mothers who keep their babies come largely from poor and deprived environments. The author discusses preventive and remedial social work with these mothers.

ROBERTS, Robert W., ed. The Unwed Mother. New York: Harper and Row, 1966.
Six sections discuss the psychological, social, and cross-cultural perspectives related to unmarried mothers.

ROWAN, Matille, and Reuben PANNOR. Casework with the Unmarried Father. New York: Child Welfare League of America, 1963.
A reprint of two papers dealing with casework related to teen-age unwed parents and the older unmarried father at the Vista Del Mar Child Care Service in Los Angeles, California.

SAUBER, Mignon, and Elaine RUBENSTEIN. Experiences of the Unmarried Mother as a Parent. New York: Community Council of Greater New York, 1965.
Initial and follow-up interviews were conducted with 321 mothers upon discharge from hospital. The focus of the study was on services rather than the adjustment of child and parent. Detailed data on the characteristics of the mothers are included.

SCHLESINGER, Benjamin. "The Unmarried Father: The Forgotten Man," Canada's Health and Welfare, XXI (January 1966), 4-8.
A review of existing American and Canadian studies related to the role of the unmarried father.

THOMAS, Rose C. "The Unmarried Parent," Public Welfare, XXIII (April 1965), 79-86.
The significance of the worker-client and supervisor-worker relationship in dealing with the unmarried parent is stressed.

TUTTLE, E. "Serving the Unmarried Mother Who Keeps Her Child," Social Casework, XLIII (October 1962), 415-422.

Suggests that Aid-to-Dependent-Children casework diagnosis involves an understanding of cultural attitudes towards illegitimacy, sexual relations, and parent-child relations in illegitimate families. Treatment should be oriented to building up clients' self-esteem and assimilation into the community.

VINCENT, Clark E. "Illegitimacy in the Next Decade: Trends and Implications," Child Welfare, XLIII (December 1964), 513-520.
The trends of illegitimacy and adoption in the United States are analyzed. Comment on solutions of this social problem is included.

--------. "Unmarried Mothers: Society's Dilemma," Sexology, XXVIII (February 1962), 452-455.
The ineffectual approaches in our society to the problem of increasing illegitimacy are reviewed.

--------. Unmarried Mothers. New York: The Free Press, 1961.
Unwed mothers are likely to be unique only to the extent that they are unwed mothers. They are representative of females throughout America.

--------. "Unmarried Fathers and the Mores: 'Sexual Exploiter' as an ex post facto Label," American Sociological Review, XXV (February 1960), 40-46.
An examination of 201 white unmarried father/unwed mother pairs. Traditional values in society apply the "sexual exploiter" label to the unmarried father. Suggestions for research in this area are listed.

WRIGHT, Helen R. 80 Unwed Mothers Who Kept Their Babies. Los Angeles: California Department of Social Welfare, 1965.
Eighty mothers who kept their children were interviewed. The report deals with the adjustment of the mother, the care of the child, and the nature of current life situations.

REMARRIAGE

BERNARD, Jessie. "Remarriage of the Widowed and
the Divorced," in Ruth S. Cavan, ed., Marriage
and the Family in the Modern World. New York:
Thomas Y. Crowell, 1960, pp. 416-424.
Potential problem areas in remarriage of the widowed
include: idealization of the deceased mate, the unsought
termination of the previous marriage, and the lack of
acceptance of the new spouse into the social matrix of
the widowed. With the divorced, and especially with the
female, guilty, jealous, paranoid, or punitive feelings
present much more serious adjustment problems if only
one of the divorced parties remarries; remarriage for
both parties comes closest to a solution.

--------. Remarriage. New York: The Dryden Press,
1956.
The only available book on remarriage. Using 2,009
cases of remarriage, it covers such areas as motiva-
tion, children, competition, conflict, and success in remarriages.

BITTERMAN, Catherine M. "The Multimarriage Family," Social Casework, XLIX (April 1968), 218-221.
Some notes on remarriage and some of the problem
areas, such as children, in a second union. Implications for caseworkers are briefly dealt with.

BOWERMAN, Charles E., and Donald IRISH. "Some
Relationships of Stepchildren to Their Parents,"
Marriage and Family Living, XXIV (May 1962),
113-121.
Homes involving step-relationships proved more likely
to have stress, ambivalence, and low cohesiveness than
did normal homes. The analysis included 2,145 stepchildren in 1953.

FAST, Irene, and Albert C. CAIN. "The Stepparent
Role: Potential for Disturbances in Family

110

Functioning, " American Journal of Orthopsychiatry,
XXVI (April 1966), 485-491.
The contradictory pressures on stepparents to act the
roles of parent, nonparent, and stepparent are discussed.

LEDEVER, Anne Rossmore. "The Stepmother: Image
and Reality, " The Single Parent, IX (May 1966),
8-9 and 44.
A stepmother of seven years shares her experiences to
illustrate the fallacy of the Cinderella legend.

MONAHAN, Thomas P. "The Changing Nature and Instability of Remarriages, " Eugenics Quarterly, V
(June 1958), 73-85.
A short review of divorce rates in American history,
with an analysis of divorce rates among second marriages in Iowa, 1953-1955.

--------. "How Stable Are Remarriages?, " American
Journal of Sociology, LVIII (November 1952), 280-
288.
An examination of marriage and divorce records in Iowa
and Missouri confirms the viewpoint that second marriages are not as enduring as first marriages.

PERRY, Joseph B., and Erdwin H. PFUHL. "Adjustment of Children in 'Solo' and 'Remarriage' Homes, "
Marriage and Family Living, XXV (May 1963), 221-
223.
This study examined 136 children living in one-parent
homes and 267 children in "remarriage" homes. No
significant differences in adjustments were reported.

PODOLSKY, Edward. "The Emotional Problems of the
Stepchild, " Mental Hygiene, XXXIV (January 1955),
49-53.
A general discussion of the special problems faced by
the stepchild and his adjustment to the new condition of
a second family.

SCHWARTZ, Anne C. "Reflections on Divorce and Remarriage." See annotation under DIVORCE.

SIMON, Anne W. Stepchild in the Family: A View of
Children in Remarriage. New York: The Odyssey
Press, 1964.
There are seven million stepchildren in the United States.
From case histories, literature, legend and history, so-
ciological and psychiatric studies, the author presents a
picture of the stepchild's world. A ten-page bibliography
is included.

SLAFF, Saul, and Vi SLAFF. "Remarriage: The Other
Side of the Coin," The Single Parent, X (January
1967), 4-7.
An examination of the meaning and uniqueness of remarriage by two remarried persons.

SMITH, William Carlson. The Stepchild. Chicago:
University of Chicago Press, 1953.
An exposition of the role and influence of stepparents,
especially the mother. It attempts to clear up some of
the misconceptions of the role of stepmother. A six-
page bibliography is included.

THOMSON, Helen. The Successful Stepparent. New
York: Harper and Row, 1966.
Offers concrete advice in relation to the problems faced
by stepparents and stepchildren. The adjustments in
remarriage are also covered.


BIBLIOGRAPHIES


ALDOUS, Joan, and Reuben HILL. International Bibliography of Research in Marriage and the Family,
1900-1964. Minneapolis: University of Minnesota
Press, 1967.

Contains international bibliographic non-annotated items related to the one-parent family.

BELL, Robert R. A Bibliography of American Family
    Problem Areas. Philadelphia: Temple University,
    Sociology Department, December 1964.
This bibliography contains 97 items related to the one-parent family up to 1964 (see pp. 25-29).

KALISH, Richard A. Death and Bereavement: An An-
    notated Social Science Bibliography. Philadelphia:
    Smith, Kline and French Laboratories, 1965.
The author has included 408 items related to death and bereavement.

SCHLESINGER, Benjamin. Poverty in Canada and the
    United States: Overview and Annotated Bibliography.
    Toronto: University of Toronto Press, 1966; re-
    printed 1968.
Under the sections of family life and child rearing,
material related to one-parent families can be found.

--------. "The One-Parent Family: Recent Literature, "
    Journal of Marriage and the Family, XXVIII
    (February 1966), 103-109.
Forty-three books, pamphlets, and articles dealing with
the one-parent family in Canada and the United States are
annotated.

--------. The Multi-Problem Family: A Review and
    Annotated Bibliography. Toronto: University of
    Toronto Press, 1965.
The 300 items on the Multi-Problem family contain
material related to the fact that many of these families
are headed by one parent, usually the mother.

ANNOTATED BIBLIOGRAPHY 1970-1974

MARRIAGE AND FAMILY

ADAMS, Bert N. The American Family: A Sociological
    Interpretation. Chicago: Markham Publishing Co., 1971.
A book which presents analytic frameworks and theoretical conceptions for organizing and interpreting the data available on
the American family.

ANDERSON, Michael, ed. Sociology of the Family. London:
    Penguin Books, 1971.
A volume of readings which concentrates on the family in the
western industrial society, and is especially concerned with
showing the diversity of family types.

ANDERSON, Wayne T. Alone But Not Lonely. Salt Lake City,
    Utah: Deseret Book Co., 1973.
Thoughts for the single, widowed, or divorced woman.

BENSON, Leonard. The Marriage Bond: Marriage, Love, and
    Sex in America. New York: Random House, 1971.
Chapters 13 and 14, pp. 265-321, deal with domestic deteriora-
tion, divorce and remarriage.

BERNARD, Jessie. Marriage and Family Among Negroes.
    Englewood Cliffs, N.J.: Prentice-Hall, 1966.
The author examines the marriage patterns of the Negroes in
America, and their influence on family life.

BRODERICK, Carlfred E., ed. A Decade of Family Research
    and Action. Minneapolis: National Council on Family
    Relations, 1972.
Fourteen reprinted articles, an inventory of family research
during 1960-1970.

BILLINGSLEY, Andrew. Black Families in White America. Englewood Cliffs, N.J.: Prentice-Hall, 1968. A historical analysis of the aspirations, structures, and problems of black families in America.

CAVAN, Ruth Shoule, ed. Marriage and Family in the Modern World; 3rd ed. New York: Thomas Y. Crowell, 1969. Sixty-four articles examine family life in the United States. Stresses in the family, as well as conflict, divorce, and readjustment, are included in this book of readings.

COSER, Rose Laub, ed. Life Cycle and Achievement in America. New York: Harper Torchbooks, 1969. Nine experts discuss class positions and role relationships from the various stages of socialization during the life cycle.

DUVALL, Evelyn Millis. Faith in Families. Chicago: Rand McNally, 1970. A guide to the pressures facing modern families in America. Explains what a modern family is, and how to deal with the problems of family life.

EDWARDS, John N., ed. The Family and Change. New York: Alfred A. Knopf, 1969. Thirty selections focus on the American family in a context of change. Areas covered include urbanization and the family, family structure and function, and some forecasts and predictions about the family in America.

ESHLEMAN, Ross J. The Family: An Introduction. Boston: Allyn and Bacon, 1974. A review of the basic concepts and ideas in marriage and the family. Chapter 17 deals with marital crisis.

ESHLEMAN, J. Ross, ed. Perspectives in Marriage and the Family: Text and Readings. Boston: Allyn and Bacon, 1969. An overview of American marriage and the family as conceptualized by Americans. Includes material on family crisis and disorganization.

115

FARBER, Bernard. Family and Kinship in Modern Society.
Glenview, Ill.: Scott, Foresman, and Co., 1973.
Chapter 2 deals with marriage and divorce.

FARMER, Mary. The Family. New York: Humanities Press,
1970.
An introduction to the sociology of the family by a British lec-
turer in social science.

FARSON, Richard E., Philip M. HAUSER, Herbert STROUP,
and Anthony J. WIENER. The Future of the Family.
New York: Family Service Association of America, 1969.
Four authors discuss the future of the American family, its
needs, and the challenges facing it as we move toward the year
2000.

FERRISS, Abbott L. Indicators of Change in the American
Family. New York: Russell Sage Foundation, 1970.
A selection of some existent and some new measures of family
change. The statistical tables include data on divorce, poverty,
marital status and households in America up to 1967.

FOLKMAN, Jerome D., and Nancy M. CLUTWORTHY.
Marriage Has Many Faces. Columbus, Ohio: Charles E.
Merrill, 1970.
A functional interdisciplinary approach to marriage in America,
using literary, historical, and illustrative narrative material.
The points of view and biases are sociological.

GOODE, William J., Elizabeth HOPKINS, and Helen M.
MCCLURE. Social Systems and Family Patterns: A Pre-
positional Inventory. New York: Bobbs and Merrill, 1971.
This compendium contains the major prepositions relating
family variables to other institutions.

GORDON, Michael, ed. The American Family in Social-
historical Perspective. New York: St. Martin's Press,
1973.
Twenty articles review the social history of American families.
Some European and English material is included to provide a

comparative perspective.

HADDEN, Jeffrey K., and Marie L. BOGATTA, eds. Marriage and the Family: A Comprehensive Reader. Itasca, Ill.: F.E. Peacock, 1969.
Sixty-five selections cover the origin of the family, family systems, contemporary family and family cycle, and selected functions in family life, including the incomplete family.

ISHWARAN, K., ed. The Canadian Family. New York: Holt, Rinehart & Winston, 1971.
Thirty selections deal with all aspects of Canadian family life including ethnicity and the family, family life styles, second marriages, kinship, and family life and mental health.

KELLEY, Robert K. Courtship, Marriage, and the Family. New York: Harcourt, Brace and World, 1969.
The first part of the book examines patterns and purposes of courtship in the United States; the second part analyzes early adjustment in marriage and subsequent family life.

KING, R.J.R., ed. Family Relations: Concepts and Theories. Berkeley, Cal.: Glendessary Press, 1969.
Nine selections provide conceptual framework for examining modern marriage and family life.

KLEMER, Richard H. Marriage and Family Relationships. New York: Harper and Row, 1970.
This book contains many case presentations that portray the realistic day-to-day experiences of marriage and family life.

LASSWELL, Marcia E., and Thomas E. LASSWELL, eds. Love, Marriage, Family: A Developmental Approach. Glenview, Ill.: Scott, Foresman and Co., 1973.
Part 13, pp. 455-502, deals with marriage dissolution and multimarriage families.

MARTINSON, Floyd Mansfield. Family in Society. New York: Dodd, Mead and Co., 1970.
This book considers in depth the family in one complex urban-

industrial society. It relates the family to other systems in American society -- the community, social class, government, the economic system, religion, and welfare.

NYE, Ivan F., and Felix M. BERARDO. The Family: Its
    Structure and Function. New York: Macmillan, 1973.
Part II, pp. 437-533, deals with family reorganization and interaction, including divorce and desertion.

OTTO, Herbert A. The Family in Search of a Future. New
    York: Appleton-Century-Crofts, 1970.
Fifteen contributors examine alternate models of family life and their implications to present family patterns.

REISS, Ira L. The Family System in America. New York:
    Holt, Rinehart and Winston, 1971.
A sociological orientation, which attempts to integrate its approach and explanation. Gives insights into the past and into the immediate future of the family in human society. Has a strong interdisciplinary flavour.

--------., ed. Readings in the Family System. New York:
    Holt, Rinehart and Winston, 1972.
Section IX, pp. 487-531, deals with marital dissolution.

RODGERS, Roy H. Family Interaction and Transaction: The
    Developmental Approach. Englewood Cliffs, N.J.:
    Prentice-Hall, 1973.
An up-to-date presentation of the developmental conceptual approach to the family.

SAXTON, Lloyd. The Individual, Marriage and the Family.
    Belmont, Calif.: Wadsworth Publishing Co., 1968.
A theoretical and practical guide to the role interaction, power structure, conflict adjustment, and need fulfilments of dating, mating, and familial relations.

SCHLESINGER, Benjamin. Families: A Canadian Perspective.
    Toronto: McGraw-Hill-Ryerson, 1972.
Unit Four, pp. 13-89, deals with the single-parent family in Canada.

SCHLESINGER, Benjamin. The Jewish Family: A Survey and
    Annotated Bibliography. Toronto: University of Toronto
    Press, 1971.
Four essays and a 430-item annotated bibliography examine the
Jewish family, including family dissolution.

SCHULZ, David A. The Changing Family. Englewood Cliffs,
    N.J.: Prentice-Hall, 1972.
An interdisciplinary approach to the family.

SKOLNICK, Arlene, and Jerome H. SKOLNICK, eds. Family
    in Transition. Boston: Little, Brown & Co., 1971.
Fifty selections examine marriage, sexuality, child bearing,
and family organization. Chapter 9 contains selections related
to the one-parent family.

TOMAN, Walter. Family Constellation; 2nd ed. New York:
    Springer Publishing Co., 1969.
The effects of one's parents and siblings on the course of one's
life are examined through extensive research studies.

WESTLEY, William A., and Nathan B. EPSTEIN. Silent
    Majority. San Francisco: Jossey-Bass Inc., 1960.
A report of two long-term psychiatric-sociological studies of
"normal" families in Montreal, Quebec, Canada.

WINCH, Robert F., and Louis Wolf GOODMAN, eds. Selected
    Studies in Marriage and the Family; 3rd ed. New York:
    Holt, Rinehart and Winston, 1968.
Sixty-two articles cover the general sociology of the family,
parent-child relationship, husband-wife relationship, including
marital dissolution.

YORBURG, Betty. The Changing Family. New York: Columbia
    University Press, 1973.
A comprehensive introduction to the basic social institution of
the family in its American context.

YOUNG, Leontine. The Fractured Family. New York:
    McGraw-Hill, 1973.

An examination of the strengths and weaknesses of the traditional American family structure. Includes discussion relating
to changes in the family.


ONE-PARENT FAMILY

## GENERAL

ADAMS, Paul L. "Functions of the Lower-class Partial
  Family", American Journal of Psychiatry, CXXX
  (February 1973), 200-203
A discussion of fatherless families in lower-class homes. Six
million children in the U.S.A. experience this type of family.

American Families: Trends and Pressures, 1973. Washington,
  D.C. Superintendent of Documents, 1974.
The hearings of the Subcommittee on Children and Youth,
Sept. 24-26, 1973 include a lot of material related to one-
parent families in the United States.

BIGNER, Jerry J. "Fathering: Research and Practice Implications", The Family Coordinator, XIX (October 1970),
  357-62.
This paper focuses on the status of the research literature on
fathering. Implications are drawn from the research findings.

BLAKE, Pamela. The Plight of One-parent Families. London:
  Council for Children's Welfare, 1972.
This booklet presents the plight of one-parent families in Britain.

BLOOD, Robert O. The Family. New York: Free Press,
  1972.
The author deals with organizational crises in the family in
Section D, pp. 542-630, in his comprehensive text-book on the
family.

BURGESS, Jane K. "The Single-Parent Family: A Social and
  Sociological Problem", The Family Coordinator, XIX
  (April 1970), 137-44.

The primary emphasis in this paper is on "marital roles" rather than the traditional "parental roles".

CANADA. Royal Commission on the Status of Women in Canada. Report. Ottawa: Information Canada, 1970.
Considerations related to the mother who heads a family are given in this report (chapters 4, 5, 6).

CANADIAN COUNCIL ON SOCIAL DEVELOPMENT. The One-Parent Family. Ottawa, 1971.
An inquiry on one-parent families in Canada, including case studies.

CHAPMAN, F. A. R. Everything You Should Know about Law and Marriage. Toronto: Burns and MacEachern Ltd., 1970.
A guide to Canadian laws related to marriage and marriage dissolution.

COWHIG, James D. "Characteristics of Families Headed by Women, March 1968". Welfare in Review, VIII (January-February 1970), 16-20.
A statistical analysis of female-headed single-parent families.

DOUGLAS, William. The One-Parent Family. Nashville, Tenn.: Graded Press, 1971 (Methodist Publishing House).
A study book in the Family Life series which discusses the particular problems and adjustments faced by single parents.

FARBER, Bernard. Family and Kinship in Modern Society. Glenview, Ill.: Scott, Foresman and Co., 1973.
Chapters 2 and 3, pp. 23-83, deal with paradigms of family and kinship implicit in modern marriages and divorce laws. The status of illegitimate children is also discussed.

FIRST, Elsa. "The First Year of Analysis of a Fatherless Boy", Journal of Child Psychotherapy, II (1970), 39-53.
A report on some clinical material from the first year of analysis of a fatherless five-year old boy.

GEORGE, Victor, and Paul WILDING. Motherless Families.

London: Routledge and Kegan Paul, 1972.
A study of 600 motherless families in East Midlands, Great
Britain. The data is based on interviews with the fathers.

GLASSER, Paul H., and Lois N. GLASSER, eds. Families
    in Crisis. New York: Harper and Row, 1970.
Part III, pp. 91-218, of this book of readings includes seven
papers on disorganization of family life.

GORE, Walter R. "The Relationship between Sex Roles,
    Marital Status and Mental Illness", Social Forces, LI
    (September 1972), 34-44.
A comparison of mental illness rates among men and women
who are single, married, divorced, and widowed.

GORNEY, Sondra, and Claire COX. After Forty. New York:
    Dial Press, 1973.
Chapter 6, pp. 135-167, deals with the woman after 40 years
who is widowed or divorced.

GOULD, Ethel. "The Single-Parent Family Benefits in Parents
    Without Partners", Journal of Marriage and the Family,
    XXX (November 1968), 666-671.
The program offered by the organization called Parents Without
Partners, Inc. is examined. Some single-parent statistics
related to the United States are included.

GUYATT, Doris. The One-Parent Family in Canada. Ottawa:
    Vanier Institute of the Family, 1971.
This comprehensive statistical analysis of single-parenthood
in Canada includes the results of a small sample study of one-
parent families.

HALLETT, Kathryn J. A T A Primer for the Single Parent.
    St. Louis, Missouri: Transactional Analysts, 1973.
A transactional analysis for single parents.

--------. "Write a Winning Script", The Single Parent, XVI
    (September 1973), 8-9.
A short description of the usefulness of transactional analysis
for the single parent.

HARTNAGEL, Timothy F. "Father Absence and Self-Conception Among Lower Class White and Negro Boys", Social Problems, XVIII (Fall 1970), 152-63.
A discussion of father absence for white and negro boys.

HERZOG, Elizabeth, and Cecelia E. SUDIA. Boys in Fatherless Families. Washington, D. C. : Children's Bureau, 1970.
A comprehensive review of studies related to father-absence. A 200-item bibliography is included in the monograph.

--------. "Family Structure and Composition: Research Considerations", in Race, Research, and Reason: Social Work Perspectives. New York: National Association of Social Workers, 1969, 145-64.
An attempt to unmask the stereotype that social scientists have managed to promote in the area of the fatherless family. The authors examine the generalizations which have been made and challenge the findings by other relevant evidence. Implications for research are included.

--------. "Fatherless Homes: A Review of the Research", Children, XV (September-October 1968), 177-82.
A summary of findings based on a review of almost 400 studies conducted during the last two decades which deal with homes where father was the absent parent.

HETHERINGTON, Mavis E. "Girls without Fathers", Psychology Today (February 1973), 47-52.
A study of 72 adolescent girls (13-17 years), of whom two-thirds lived in one-parent families without fathers. Father-absence appeared to show up in a girl's behaviour in adolescence.

JAMES, Jean M. Family-Benefit Mothers in Metropolitan Toronto. Toronto: Ministry of Community and Social Services, 1973.
In 1970 there were almost 65,000 recipients of Family Benefits in Ontario. The study examines in detail 414 women who are under this programme.

KADUSHIN, Alfred. "Single-Parent Adoptions: An Overview
    and Some Relevant Research", Social Service Review, XLIV
    (September 1970), 263-274.
This article reviews the problems and advantages of single-
parent adoptions, as well as the relevant research.

KEYSERLING, Mary Dublin. Windows on Day Care. New
    York: National Council of Jewish Women, 1972.
A full discussion of day care needs and problems in the United
States, with special emphasis on one-parent families.

KOGELSCHATZ, Joan L., Paul L. ADAMS, and Daniel McK.
    TUCKER. "Family Styles of Fatherless Households",
    Journal of the American Academy of Child Psychiatry, II
    (1972), 365-383.
A study of 105 children whose fathers were not living at home.
Two groups were examined: The "transitional" fatherless group
whose fathers were absent for two years or less, and the "hard
core" group whose fathers were absent for more than two years.

KOPT, Kathryn E. "Family Variables and School Adjustment
    of Eighth Grade Father-Absent Boys", The Family Co-
    ordinator, XIX (April 1970), 145-150.
An explorative study of the school adjustment of boys in father-
absent homes.

KRIESBERG, Louis. Mothers in Poverty: A Study of Father-
    less Families. Chicago: Aldine Publishing Co., 1970.
An in-depth study of women-headed families in public housing
projects in Syracuse.

KRONBY, Malcolm C. The Guide to Family Law. Toronto:
    New Press, 1972.
A Canadian family-law lawyer explains in simple language the
present law dealing with separation, divorce, and allied family
legal matters.

LASSWELL, Marcia E., and Thomas E. LASSWELL, eds.
    Love, Marriage, Family: A Developmental Approach.
    Glenview, Ill.: Scott, Foresman and Co., 1973.

Part 13, pp. 455-501, has six selections dealing with widow-hood, divorce, remarriage, and stepparents. These are all reprints from journals and books.

LAW REFORM COMMITTEE OF CANADA. The Family Court. Ottawa: Information Canada, 1974.
This is a working paper of the Law Reform Committee of Canada, and deals with all aspects related to the family court which is involved in many facets of the legal problems of one-parent families.

LEMASTERS, E.E. Parents in Modern America. Homewood, Ill.: Dorsey Press, 1970.
Chapter 9, pp. 157-175, discusses the topic of parents without partners.

LYMAN, Howard. Single Again. New York: David McKay Co., 1971.
A psychologist gives practical advice to the newly divorced or widowed man or woman.

--------. "A Successful Community Project for 'Single Agains'", The Single Parent, XV (March 1972), 5-9.
A psychology professor describes the content of an evening course for adults who were "single again".

MARSDEN, Dennis. Mothers Alone: Poverty and the Father-less Family. London: Allen Lane, Penguin Press, 1969.
A study of 116 British one-parent mothers who were all on National Assistance (welfare).

NEWMAN, Gustave, and Sydney B. DENMAN. "Felony and Paternal Deprivation: A Socio-Psychiatric View", International Journal of Social Psychiatry, XVII (Winter 1970-71), 65-71.
An examination of 49 male white prisoners in Florida and a review of their fatherless family background.

PARENTS WITHOUT PARTNERS. The Best from the Single Parent. Washington, D.C., 1973.

Thirty-nine articles are reprinted from the journal, The Single
Parent.

PECK, Bruce B. "Psychotherapy with Fragmented Father-
    Absent Families", Family Therapy II (June 1974), 27-42.
A discussion of one-parent families in therapy, and some of
their problems which emerge in treatment.

PEITCHINIS, S.G. The Employability of Welfare Recipients.
    Edmonton: Human Resources Research Council of Alberta,
    1972.
A total of 1,310 files were examined from welfare records
(1,044 active, 226 inactive). Mothers with dependent children
accounted for almost 58% of all women on welfare.

POLLAK, Gertrude K. "Sexual Dynamics of Parents without
    Partners", Social Work XV (April 1970), 79-85.
A report of some of the social-sexual adjustment problems
faced by single-parents. The information was obtained from
seminar groups conducted by the Family Service of Philadelphia.

REID, William J., and Audrey D. SMITH. "AFDC Mothers
    View the Work Incentive Program", Social Service Review,
    XLVI (September 1972), 347-362.
A study of 318 AFDC mothers of whom 90 per cent were slack
about their attitudes toward the Work Incentive Program.

ROSENBERG, Morris. "The Broken Family and Self-Esteem",
    in Readings on the Family System, ed. by Ira L. Reiss.
    New York: Holt, Rinehart and Winston, 1972, 518-530.
A study of children in intact and broken families, and resultant
emotional disturbances in various families, typified by religion
and marital status.

ROSENFELD, Jona M., and Eliezer ROSENSTEIN. "Towards
    a Conceptual Framework for the Study of Parent-Absent
    Families", Journal of Marriage and the Family, XXXV
    (February 1973), 131-135.
A mapping system is presented which distinguishes between
six facets concerning the nature of the absence of one parent in

families. It can be used as a framework for research on one-parent families.

SCHLESINGER, Benjamin. One-Parent Families in Canada.
Toronto: Guidance Centre, Faculty of Education,
University of Toronto, 1974.
This booklet highlights the facts, problems, and reports
related to one-parent families in Canada.

--------. "The One-Parent Family in Canada: Some Recent
Findings and Recommendations", The Family Coordinator,
XXII (July 1973), 305-309.
Two major 1971 reports on Canadian one-parent families are
summarized.

SHERMAN, Edward A., Michael H. PHILLIPS, Barbara L.
HARING, and Ann W. SHYNE. Service to Children in
Their Own Homes: Its Nature and Outcome. New York:
Child Welfare League of America, 1973.
A study of 246 families of whom 61% were one-parent families.
The study examines in detail home service for the families.

STEIRMAN COMMUNICATIONS. Single.
New York, 1973.
A special magazine for the unmarried, widowed, divorced, and
unattached. (Vol. I, No. I, started August 1973).

SUDIA, Cecelia E. "An Updating and Comment on the United
States Scene", The Family Coordinator, XXII (July 1973),
309-311.
A short statistical presentation of one-parent families in the
United States in 1971.

TAVES, Isabella. Women Alone. New York: Funk and
Wagnalls, 1969.
A practical handbook for widows and divorcees. Some of the
information is based on questionnaires.

THOMAS, Mary Margaret. "Children with Absent Fathers",
Journal of Marriage and the Family, XXX (February 1968),

89-96.
The role of the father in socializing children was examined by
studying effects of his absence on nine- to eleven-year-old
boys and girls.

TUNNEY, John V. "You've Been Singled Out!", The Single
    Parent, XV (April 1972), 3-5.
Senator John Tunney discusses how American income tax laws
discriminate against single parents who must work.

UNITED NATIONS. Parental Rights and Duties, Including
    Guardianship. New York, 1968.
Chapters III and IV deal with broken families and mothers as
sole parents.

UNITED STATES. Department of Health, Education, and
    Welfare. Findings of the 1971 AFDC Study, Part I.
    Washington, D.C.: Social and Rehabilitation Service, 1971.
This study deals with the demographic and program characteristics of families who received assistance payment in January
1971 (2,523,900 families).

VAYHINGER, John M. The Single Parent Family. Nashville,
    Tennessee: Board of Education, Methodist Church, 1972.
    (P.O. Box 871, Nashville, Tenn., 37202)
This pamphlet reviews the statistics in the U.S.A. related to
single-parent families, and discusses the role of the church
related to this problem.

WEISS, Robert S. "The Contributions of an Organization of
    Single Parents to the Well-Being of Its Members", The
    Family Coordinator, XXII (July 1973), 321-326.
A discussion of the contribution of one chapter of "Parents
Without Partners" to its members.

WEISS, Robert S. Loneliness. The Experience of Emotional
    and Social Isolation. Cambridge: Massachusetts Institute
    of Technology Press, 1974.
A discussion of emotional and social isolation.

# DIVORCED

ABRAXAS CORPORATION. Marriage and Divorce. Los
Angeles, 1974.
A new popular journal, dealing with marriage and divorce.
Published 6 times per year.

ACKERMAN, Nathan W. "Divorce and Alienation in Modern
Society," Mental Hygiene, LIII (January 1969), 118-127.
A theoretical examination of the place of divorce in modern
society, with a suggested program of prevention. The author
raises certain questions which will have to be examined through
extensive research.

ARLEN, Michael J. "Saturday Father," The Single Parent,
XVI (May 1973), 6-8.
A divorced father discusses his feelings on visiting his children
who are living with the mother.

BLOCK, Jean Libman. Back in Circulation. New York:
Macmillan, 1969.
A divorced woman discusses the practical aspects of living as
a divorcee, including parent-child relations.

BOHANAN, Paul, ed. Divorce and After. New York: Doubleday,
1970.
Eleven selections deal with an analysis of the emotional and
social problems of divorce.

BRISCOE, William C., James B. SMITH, Eli ROBINS, Sue
MARTEN, and Fred GASKIN. "Divorce and Psychiatric
Disease," Archives of General Psychiatry, XXIX (July
1973), 119-125.
A psychiatric study of 139 divorced men and women and a
control group to determine the incidence and relationship to
psychiatric illness to marital turmoil and divorce.

CARTER, Hugh, and Paul C. GLICK. Marriage and Divorce:
A Social and Economic Study. Cambridge, Mass.:
Harvard University Press, 1970.

129

A comprehensive examination of the social and economic aspects of marriage, divorce, and widowhood.

CHEN, Ronald. "The Dilemma of Divorce: Disaster or Remedy," The Family Coordinator, XVII (October 1968), 251-255.
This short view of the SOS program developed in California, a "mutual aid" type of organization for recent divorced adults, deals also with types of marital relationships which tend to lead to divorce.

COLTON, Helen. "Sex Problems of the Single Parent", in her Sex after the Revolution. New York: Association Press, 1972, 207-225.
A family life teacher discusses the area of sexuality as related to divorced women.

COSNECK, Bernard J. "Divorce after Fifteen Years", The Single Parent, XV (February 1972), 13-15.
A study of 173 men and women who were divorced after an average of 20 years of marriage.

COSNECK, Bernard J. "What about the Effects of Divorce?" The Single Parent, XVI (March 1973), 6-10.
A discussion of the effects of divorce on children, based on a sample of 173 questionnaires to single parents (27 men, 146 women).

CULL, John C., and Richard E. HARDY, eds. Deciding on Divorce: Personal and Family Considerations. Springfield, Ill.: Charles C. Thomas, 1974.
The ten contributors discuss some of the goals and dimensions of marriage counselling related to whether a marriage can or cannot be saved.

DEWOLFE, Rose. The Bonds of Acrimony. New York: Lippincott, 1970.
Amusing, accurate and unpleasant anecdote about divorced people.

DRANOV, Paula. "What Every Agency Should Know about 'No-Fault' Divorce", Human Needs, I (April-May 1973), 26-28. A good summary of the new no-fault divorce clause, and some of the legal implications involved in settlements under this clause.

FISHER, Esther Oshiver. "A Guide to Divorce Counselling", The Family Coordinator, XXII (January 1973), 55-61. This article discusses pre-divorce, divorce, and post-divorce counselling as a new approach to dealing with divorce.

FREID, Jacob, ed. Jews and Divorce. New York: KTAV Publishing House, 1968. A collection of the papers given at a conference to discuss the problems related to divorce among Jews in America.

FULLER, Jan. Space: The Scrap book of My Divorce. New York: Arthur Fields Books Inc., 1973. A three months' diary-like journal starting with the day her divorce became final.

GARDNER, Richard A. The Boys and Girls Book about Divorce. New York: Bantam Books, 1971. An advice-giving book related to how to help children in a divorce.

--------. "Reactions to Divorce by the Children", The Single Parent, XVI (November 1973), 3-5 (Part I). Part II, XVI (December 1973) 3-7. A discussion of how children feel towards divorce.

GREEN, Bernard. "The Divorce Act of 1968", University of Toronto Law Journal, XIX (1969), 627-641. A legal analysis of the new Canadian divorce act by a family law professor.

GROLLMAN, Earl A., ed. Explaining Divorce to Children. Boston: Beacon Press, 1969. Ten contributors examine divorce and the effect on children from a sociological, psychological, and religious point of view.

131

HIRSCH, Barbara. Divorce for Women. Chicago: Henry
    Regnery, 1973.
The legal and administrative aspects of divorce are reviewed
in this book.


HUDSON, Lufter R. 'Til Divorce Do Us Part. Nashville,
    Tenn.: Thomas Nelson, 1973.
A counsellor offers help to married persons who feel the
necessity of breaking a marriage.


KINDER, Melvin. "Divorce: Does it Really Mean Failure?",
    The Single Parent, XVII (June 1974), 15-18.
A discussion in which the author sees divorce as a positive
force.


KRANTZLER, Mel. Creative Divorce. New York: M. Evans
    Co., 1973.
A California divorce therapist offers a positive program for
healing the trauma of a failed marriage.


KRISHNAN, P., and Ashraf K. KAYANI. "Estimates of Age
    Specific Divorce Rates for Females in the United States,
    1960-1969", Journal of Marriage and the Family, XXXVI
    (February 1974), 72-75.
This paper is an attempt to develop estimates of age specific
incidence of divorce for the United States female population
employing regression analyses.


LEVINE, Marcia W. "New Family Structures: Challenges to
    Family Casework", Journal of Jewish Communal Service,
    L (Spring 1974), 238-244.
A family agency's approach to divorced and reconstituted
families.


LOBSENZ, Norman. "How Divorced Young Mothers Learn to
    Stand Alone", The Single Parent, XIV (December 1971),
    3-6.
A journalist interviews divorced mothers, and discusses some
of their problems and how they cope with them.

MATZKIN, William L. "Contested Divorce: Legal Fiction versus Emotional Reality", The Single Parent XVI (April 1973), 6-8.
A discussion of the application of divorce law to domestic relations by a psychiatrist.

MELMAN, Carla. "Divorce: A Community Affair", The Single Parent XVII (April 1974), 8-12.
A discussion of the involvement of various community members in divorce.

MESSER, Alfred A. "Dissolution of Long-Standing Marriages," Mental Hygiene, LIII (January 1969), 127-130.
A general discussion of the increasing divorces which occur after 15 years of marriage. The author raises many questions regarding this phenomenon.

MINDEY, Carol. The Divorced Mother. New York: McGraw-Hill, 1970.
The author, who was divorced and remarried after seven years of being a "parent without a partner," offers advice to those who find themselves in the divorced group.

MONAHAN, Thomas P. "National Divorce Legislation: The Problem and Some Suggestions", The Family Coordinator, XXII (July 1973), 353-357.
An account of the efforts of the National Conference of Commissioners on Uniform State Laws to develop a uniform code for marriage and divorce.

O'BRIEN, John E. "Violence in Divorce-Prone Families", Journal of Marriage and the Family, XXXIII (November 1971), 692-698.
A study of 25 violent and 125 non-violent families. The examination of spouses in a divorce action revealed a significant incidence of violent family behaviour.

PALMER, Sally E. "Reasons for Marriage Breakdown: A Case Study in Southwestern Ontario, Canada", Journal of Comparative Family Studies II (Autumn 1971), 251-262.

A study of 291 divorcing couples with children, who started divorce proceedings during a two and a half year old period. The findings were compared to married couples who were not planning divorce.

PUBLIC HEALTH SERVICE. Children of Divorced Couples: United States, Selected Years. Washington, D. C., 1970. In recent years about nine children out of every 1,000 representing over one-half million children, have been involved each year in divorces. Statistics for the periods 1922-32 and 1950-65 are analyzed.

RHEINSTEIN, Max. Marriage Stability, Divorce and the Law. Chicago: University of Chicago Press, 1972. Explores the history and present status of divorce law and marriage stability in Japan, Italy, Sweden, France, the Soviet Union and the United States.

ROBBINS, Norman N. "End of Divorce - Beginning of Legal Problems", The Family Life Coordinator, XXIII (April 1974), 185-188. An attorney discusses some of the legal aspects following a divorce action.

--------. "Have We Found Fault in No Fault Divorce?", The Family Coordinator, XXII (July 1973), 359-362. A discussion of the "No Fault" divorce laws.

ROSE, Vicki L., and Sharon PRICE-BONHAM. "Divorce Adjustment: A Woman's Problem?" The Family Coordinator, XXII (July 1973), 291-297. A review of the research on post-divorce adjustment and the major findings are presented.

ROSOW, Irving, and K. Daniel ROSE. "Divorce among Doctors", Journal of Marriage and the Family, XXXIV (November 1972), 587-598. An examination of the divorce rates in 1968 of doctors in California. The findings indicate that doctors have very low divorce rates.

RUE, James J., and Louise SHANAHAN. The Divorced
    Catholic. New York: Paulist Press, 1972.
What divorce means to Catholics.


SANCTUARY, Gerald, and Constance WHITEHEAD. Divorce
    and After. London: Penguin Handbook, 1972.
Practical advice for British families, in case divorce is
pending in their lives. Geared to giving information.


SCHLESINGER, Benjamin. "The Death of a Marriage", The
    Single Parent, XVII (May 1974), 10-12.
A discussion of divorce and remarriage.


SHERESKY, Norman, and Marya MANNES. Uncoupling: The
    Art of Coming Apart. New York: Viking Press, 1972.
A discussion on what happens in divorce courts.


STEINMETZ, Suzanne K., and Murray A. STRAUS, eds.
    Violence in the Family. New York: Dodd, Mead and Co.,
    1974.
Among the 38 selections three deal with violence related to
divorce in families.


STEINZOR, Bernard. When Parents Divorce. New York:
    Pocket Books, 1970.
A psychologist gives advice to parents and children related to
problems emanating from divorce.


SUGAR, Max. "Children of Divorce", Pediatrics, XLVI
    (October 1970), 588-595.
A description of some of the recurrent problems and feelings
of children involved in a divorce. Twenty-six children were
examined in the Child-Adolescent Psychiatric Out-Patient Clinic
of the Louisiana State University Medical Centre.


TASK FORCE ON DIVORCE AND DIVORCE REFORM. Task
    Force Report: Divorce and Divorce Reform, Minneapolis:
    National Council on Family Relations, 1973.
A study of divorce in the United States, and recommendations
for action. The report includes an appendix which consists of

a bibliography, reports, tapes, and testimony. United States
Senate.

VANIER INSTITUTE OF THE FAMILY. Conciliation: A Seminar
on the Law and Social Services as Applied to Divorce Proceedings in Canada. Ottawa, 1974.
This booklet summarizes an interdisciplinary seminar held in
January 1973 on the topic of conciliation prior to divorce.

VAYHINGER, John. Before Divorce. New York: Fortress
Press, 1972.
An advice-giving book related to examining marital conflicts
prior to divorce.

WRENN, Lawrence G., ed. Divorce and Remarriage in the
Catholic Church. New York: Newman Press, 1973.
Ten authors discuss the moral-religious and social aspects of
divorce and remarriage in the Catholic context.


REMARRIED

BAER, Jean. The Second Wife. New York: Doubleday,
1972.
The author interviewed 220 women who were in a second marriage. The book is primarily an advice-giving type of document.

COHEN, Sarah Betsy, and James A. SWEET. "The Impact of
Marital Disruption and Remarriage on Fertility", Journal
of Marriage and the Family, XXXVI (February 1974), 87-
96.
An examination of the relationship of marital stability and fertility using data from the 1965 U.S. National Fertility study.

FUDGE, David G. Remarriage of Divorced Persons: Research
Findings and the Possibility of a Canadian Study. Ottawa:
Vanier Institute of the Family, 1969.
A summary of available data related to the remarriages of
divorced persons, and a research proposal for a study on re-
marriage and divorce in Canada.

GROSSMAN, Bruce C., and William T. HIEBERT. "Preparation for Remarriage", The Single Parent, XIV (April 1971), 31-32.
A discussion of how to prepare for subsequent remarriage.

KELLEHER, Stephen J. Divorce and Remarriage for Catholics. New York: Doubleday, 1973.
The author presents a concise statement of the Roman Catholic Church's position related to divorce and remarriage.

MARTIN, John R. Divorce and Remarriage. Scottsdale, Pa.: Herald Press, 1973.
The first part of this book gives counselling perspectives and the second focuses on the task of counselling those whose marriage has failed.

MCKAIN, Walter C. Retirement Marriage. Storrs: University of Connecticut, Storrs Agricultural Experiment Station, 1969.
Interviews were conducted with 100 couples who had remarried, where the brides were at least 60 years of age and the grooms at least 65 years of age, to trace the development of these late second marriages.

MOORE, Peter. "Enjoying the Eccentric Family", The Single Parent, XV (July-August 1972), 5-7.
The case against remarriage is discussed by a Canadian psychiatrist.

SCHLESINGER, Benjamin. "Adjustment in Remarriage", Australian Social Work, XXV (September 1972), 18-25.
A discussion of adjustment in remarrying of 96 Canadian couples.

--------. "Canadian Men Who Married for the Second Time", The Family Life Educator, 4 (March 1973), 6-7.
Characteristics of 65 men who married for the second time.

--------. "Canadian Women Who Married for the Second Time", The Family Life Educator, 4 (June 1973), 6-8.

Characteristics of 68 women who married for the second time.

--------. "Remarriage and Children", Australian Social Work,
     XXV (June 1972), 17-22.
The findings of a Canadian study on remarriage of 96 couples,
in relation to their children.

--------. "Remarriage as Family Reorganization for Divorced
     Persons: A Canadian Study", Journal of Comparative
     Family Studies, I (Autumn 1970), 100-118.
The findings of a Canadian study on remarriage covering 90
divorced persons are presented in this paper.

--------. "The Single Woman in Remarriage", Social Science
A sample of 28 single women who, married to men who were
married before, discuss remarriage.

SCHLESINGER, Benjamin, and Alex MACRAE. "Remarriages
     in Canada: Statistical Trends", Journal of Marriage and
     the Family, XXXII (May 1970), 300-303.
An overview of the statistical trends related to remarriage
(1950-64) in Canada.

--------. "The Widow and Widower in Remarriage", Omega,
     II (1971), 10-18.
A discussion of findings of a study of widows and widowers who
remarried.

SCHLESINGER, Benjamin, and Eugene STASIUK. "Children
     of Divorced Persons in Remarriage", in Children of Sepa-
     ration and Divorce, ed. by I. Stuart and L. Abt, New York:
     Grossman, 1972, 19-36.
Case material dealing with children from previously divorced
parents who were involved in second marriages.

SCHULMAN, Gerda L. "Myths That Intrude on the Adaptation
     of the Stepfamily", Social Casework, LIII (March 1972),
     131-139.
Family therapy, prior to remarriage or afterward, enables
the family to move into "unity".

TYBRING, Jane B. "Remarriage: Parenting Someone Else's
Children", The Single Parent, XVII (June 1974), 19-20, 27.
About one in nine children is a stepchild. The author discusses
the involvement of children in a second marriage.


SEPARATED

BAGUEDOR, Eve. Separation Journal of a Marriage. New
York: Simon and Schuster, 1972.
A woman describes her experiences after the break-up of her
marriage.

CANADIAN COUNCIL ON SOCIAL DEVELOPMENT. A Study
of Family Desertion in Canada. Ottawa, 1970.
A study related to data obtained in the summer of 1968 dealing
with the problem of family desertion.

CRUMLEY, Frank E., and Ronald S. BLUMENTHAL. "Children's Reactions to Temporary Loss of the Father",
American Journal of Psychiatry, CXXX (July 1973), 778-
782.
A study of 200 children during 1969-1970, whose fathers had
forced separations from their families due to military service.

PEARLMAN, Chester A. "Separation Reactions of Married
Women," American Journal of Psychiatry, CXXVI (January
1970), 70-74.
The author describes the types of reactions to periodic separation of 485 married women, all of whom were patients in an out-
patient department of a psychiatric hospital.

SKARSTEN, Stan. "Family Desertion in Canada", The Family
Coordinator, XXIII (January 1974), 19-26.
An overview of the problem of desertion in Canada. Includes
some statistical trends, and discussion of causes for discussion.

BAIZERMAN, Michael, Cynthia SHEEHAN, David L. ELLISON, and Edward R. SCHLESINGER. Pregnant Adolescents: A Review of Literature with Abstracts, 1960-1970. Washington, D.C.: Consortium on Early Child Bearing and Child Rearing, 1971.
A comprehensive annotated bibliography and review of pregnant adolescent mothers. Includes items on existing services, psychological, physical, social, and educational aspects of adolescent pregnancy.

BERNSTEIN, Rose. Helping Unmarried Mothers. New York: Association Press, 1971.
A comprehensive guide for the varied human welfare workers who come in contact with unmarried mothers. This book covers the most current practices and methods.

CRELLIN, Eilleen, et al. Born Illegitimate: Social and Education Implications. New York: Humanities Press, 1971.
A survey of 650 children in Great Britain born in the same week in 1958 and followed up until age seven.

CROMWELL, Ronald E., and Joan L. GANGEL. "A Social Action Program Directed to Sinlge Pregnant Girls and Adolescent Girls", The Family Coordinator, XXIII (January 1974), 61-66.
An urban community's action program directed to single pregnant girls is described.

CRUICKSHANK, D.A. "Forgotten Fathers: The Plight of the Putative Father in Canada", Reports of Family Law, VII (October 1973), 1-61, part 1.
A comprehensive overview of the legal aspects related to the father of an illegitimate child in Canada.

CUMISKEY, Ann Patricia, and Helen Patricia MUDD. "Postpartum Group Therapy with Unwed Mothers", Child Welfare, LI (April 1972), 241-246.
A report on the use of group method with unmarried mothers in

northern Virginia. The median age of the girls was 20, and their babies had been born prior to entering the group.

DAVIS, Hermione G., and Esther FINKEL. "The Single Parent: A Growing Challenge to Communal Service", Journal of Jewish Communal Service, L (Spring 1974), 251-256.
Casework treatment of the single parent at the Jewish Community Services of Long Island, New York.

DUKETTE, Rita, and Nicholas STEVENSON. "The Legal Rights of Unmarried Fathers: The Impact of Recent Court Decisions," Social Science Review, LXVII (March 1973), 1-15.
The issue of legal rights of out-of-wedlock fathers to their children is discussed.

EGGERS, Oscar R., ed. Unwed Parenthood: A Selected Annotated Bibliography. Kansas City: University of Missouri, Family Study Center, 1969.
Contains 154 selected annotated items dealing with American unmarried mothers and fathers.

FESTINGER, Trudy Bradley. "Unwed Mothers and Their Decisions to Keep or Surrender Children", Child Welfare, L (May 1971), 253-263.
A study of unwed women serviced by the Louise Wise Services, a voluntary social agency in New York. The characteristics of the clients, family, putative fathers, and decision-making about their babies are described and discussed.

GEGGEL, Elizabeth, and Ruth L. SCHWARTZ. "Helping the Single Mother through the Group Process", Journal of Jewish Communal Service, L (spring 1974), 245-250.
In 1972, the Jewish Family Service of Philadelphia serviced 5634 one-parent families. A description of treatment through the group process is discussed in this paper.

HOLMAN, Robert. Unsupported Mothers and the Care of Their Children. London: Mothers in Action, 1972.
A British study of 95 single-parent female-headed families.

HOWARD, Marion, and Lucy EDDINGER. Beginning a Program for Pregnant School-Age Girls. Washington, D.C.: Consortium on Early Child Bearing and Child Rearing, 1972. (Information Series No. 1).
The first of four booklets which deal with the educational, financial, legal, and service aspects of handling the pregnant school girl who plans to keep her child.

KLEIN, Carole. The Single Parent Experience. New York: Walker and Co., 1973.
A guide to men and women who raise children outside of marriage.

MACKEY, Betsy, and Margaret MILLOY. "The Impact of Teenage Pregnancy on the Professional Educator", The Family Coordinator, XXIII (January 1974), 15-18.
A discussion of the educational system and its acceptance and rejection of teenage pregnant students.

NATIONAL COUNCIL ON ILLEGITIMACY. The Double Jeopardy - The Triple Crisis: Illegitimacy Today. New York: 1969.
The problem of illegitimacy, including therapy for unmarried mothers, particularly teenage mothers, and services offered to them, are examined by eleven authors.

--------. Effective Services for Unmarried Parents and Their Children. New York: 1968.
Ten authors review services to the unwed father and unwed mother, and describe some model American programs in the area of unwed parents.

NELSON, Shirley A. "School-Age Parents", Children Today (March-April 1973), 31-33, 4.
A discussion of the pregnant schoolgirl and results of some research projects on this topic.

OSOFSKY, Howard J., and Joy D. OSOFSKY. "Adolescents as Mothers", American Journal of Orthopsychiatry, XL (October 1970), 825-834
A discussion of the medical, educational, and social problems of low-income pregnant adolescents.

142

PANNOR, Reuben, Fred MASSARIK, and Byron EVANS. The
    Unmarried Father. New York: Springer Publishing Co.,
    1971.
This study included 222 unmarried mothers and 96 unmarried
fathers at the Vista Del Mar Child-Care Service in Los Angeles.
The focus is on the social-personal-psychological characteristics of the unmarried father.

PAPADEMETRIEU, Marguerite. "Use of a Group Technique
    with Unwed Mothers and Their Families", Social Work,
    XVI (October 1971), 85-89.
Group techniques to deal with middle class unwed mothers and
their parents.

PELLKEY, Kathryn, and Elizabeth MARSH. "The Single Parent
    Enigma", Our Children, Vol. X (Summer 1973), 3-5.
A short report on a study of 39 girls who kept their children
after giving birth out of wedlock.

PIERCE, Ruth I. Single and Pregnant. Boston: Beacon Press,
    1970.
An advice-giving book to the single girl who find herself pregnant. Sources of help for such girls are included in the appendix.

POZSONYI, Judith. A Longitudinal Study of Unmarried Mothers
    Who Kept Their First-Born Children. London, Ontario:
    Family and Children's Services of London and Middlesex,
    1973.
A sample of 52 unmarried mothers was studied in 1969-70.
The study examined how these women fared in the community,
and examines the adjustment of their children.

RAINS, Prudence Mors. Becoming an Unwed Mother: A Socio-
    logical Account. Chicago: Aldine Atherton, 1971.
This study examines the actual situation of unwed motherhood,
as opposed to the causes and pathology of deviance.

SAUBER, Mignon, and Eileen M. CORRIGAN. The Six-Year
    Experience of Unwed Mothers as Parents. New York:

Community Council of Greater New York, 1970.
A longitudinal study of 200 women who kept and reared their first-born children out of wedlock.

SINGER, Ann. "A Program for Young Mothers and Their
    Babies", Social Casework, LII (November 1971), 567-577.
Practical intervention to help stabilize the lives of mothers
and their babies.

UNITED NATIONS. The Status of the Unmarried Mother: Law
    and Practice. New York, 1971 (E/CN. 6/540/Rev. 1).
A summary of the legal and social aspects related to unmarried
mothers in various countries of the world.

--------. Study of Discrimination Against Persons Born Out
    Of Wedlock. New York, 1967 (Sales No. E68 XIV 3).
A comprehensive review of the legal, social and psychological
factors related to discrimination against persons born out of
wedlock.

WILLIAMS, Tannis M. "Childrearing Practices of Young
    Mothers", American Journal of Orthopsychiatry, XLIV
    (January 1974), 70-75.
Some comments about the childrearing practices of single women
who keep their children. Discusses the lack of research on
single parents and multiple care givers and suggests directions
for study.


WIDOWED

ABRAHAMS, Ruby Banks. "Mutual Help for the Widowed",
    Social Work, XVII (September 1972), 54-61.
"The Widowed Service Line", a mutual program in Boston, is
described. This is a telephone service.

AGREE, Rose H., and Norman J. ACKERMAN. "Why Children
    Must Mourn", Marriage, LV (September 1973), 55-59.
A short discussion of dealing with death with children.

144

BERARDO, Felix M. "Survivorship and Social Isolation: The
   Case of the Aged Widower", The Family Coordinator, XIX
   (January 1970), 11-25.
Research findings related to the urban aged widower and the
difficulties he experiences are reviewed here. Social isolation
is one of the major conditions found in this population.

COSNECK, J. "Family Patterns of Older Widowed Jewish
   People", The Family Coordinator, XIX (October 1970),
   368-373.
An interview study of family patterns of widowed Jewish people
over the age of 60. The subjects consisted of 29 men and 74
women, all widowed.

GROLLMAN, Earl A., ed. Explaining Death to Children.
   Boston: Beacon Press, 1967.
The effect of death on children is examined by ten authors, who
view the topic from a cultural, sociological, psychological, and
theological point of view.

HARVEY, Carol D., and Howard M. BAHR. "Widowhood,
   Morale, and Affiliation", Journal of Marriage and the Family,
   XXXVI (February 1974), 97-106.
Data from surveys in five nations are examined in an assessment
of the attitudes and affiliation ties of widowed and married per-
sons.

KLIMAN, Gilbert. Psychological Emergencies in Childhood.
   New York: Grune and Stratton, 1968.
Pages 59-101 deal with the effects on children of death in the
family, divorce, and marital separation discussed by a psychiatrist.

KOOIMAN, Gladys. When Death Takes a Father. Grand Rapids,
   Michigan: Baker Book House, 1974. (Association Press)
A personal account of a widow and her struggles to find a home
for her eight fatherless children.

KÜBLER-ROSS, Elizabeth. On Death and Dying. New York:
   Macmillan, 1969.

145

An analysis of what the dying have to teach the helping professions and their own families in the area of the meaning of death.

LOPATA, Helena Znaniecki. "Living through Widowhood",
    Psychology Today, VII (July 1973), 87-92.
A study of 301 widows, 50 years of age and over, who live in
Metropolitan Chicago.

--------. "Loneliness: Forms and Components", Social Prob-
    lems, XVII (Fall 1969), 248-262.
The article examines the forms and components of loneliness
as experienced by widows living in an American metropolis.

--------. Widowhood in an American City. Morriston, New
    Jersey: General Learning Press, 1973.
A study of 301 widows in an urban American city.

REED, Elizabeth L. Helping Children with the Mystery of
    Death. Nashville, Tennessee: Abingdon Press, 1970.
Information for parents, teachers, ministers, relatives, and
other adults who must help children face death. The author
stresses the importance of honesty in dealing with the subject
and of preparing the child beforehand to understand the actual
experience of death.

SALOM, Francine. "Surviving Widowhood", The Single Parent,
    XVII (May 1974), 13-15.
A widow discusses how she coped with her widowhood after 22
years of marriage.

SCHLESINGER, Benjamin. "The Widowed as a One-Parent
    Family Unit", Social Science, XLVI (January 1971), 26-32.
Widows constitute the largest category of one-parent families
in the United States and Canada. Some of the results of a
Canadian study are discussed in this paper.

SCHOENBERG, Bernard, Arthur C. CARR, David PERETZ,
    and Austin H. KUTSCHER, eds. Loss and Grief. New
    York: Columbia University Press, 1973.
The effects of death and dying on both adults and children are
included in this volume.

146

SILVERMAN, Phyllis Rolfe. "The Widow as a Caregiver in a
Program of Preventive Intervention with Other Widows",
Mental Hygiene, LIV (October 1970), 540-547.
The author discusses the use of a self-help group in preventive
intervention. A group of widows reaches out to recently widowed
women and offers support in their adjustment to a new life.

--------. "The Widow to Widow Program", Mental Hygiene,
LIII (July 1969), 333-337.
A preventive program which utilizes widows as "aides" to
visit new widows and help them in their early grief. The paper
reports the results of the work of these aides with 64 widows.

START, Clarissa. On Becoming a Widow. New York: Family
Library Pyramid Publications, 1973.
A personal account of becoming a widow, including reactions
to loss and bereavement.

SWITZER, David K. The Dynamics of Grief. Nashville,
Tennessee: Abingdon Press, 1970.
This book discusses the dynamics of grief, offering improved
means for helping the bereaved, suggesting conscious preparations for grief before it begins.

TORRIE, Margaret. Begin Again. London: J. M. Dent and
Sons, 1970.
There are three million widows in Britain today. This book is
an advice-giving approach to widowhood.

VERNICK, Joel J. Selected Bibliography on Death and Dying.
Washington, D. C.: National Institute on Health, 1970.
A 1494-item bibliography which includes many references to
widowhood.


BIBLIOGRAPHIES

MINNESOTA COUNCIL ON FAMILY RELATIONS. Family Life
Literature and Films: An Annotated Bibliography, 1972.
Minneapolis, Minn., 1973.

A comprehensive bibliography of published materials and films dealing with all aspects of the family.

VANIER INSTITUTE OF THE FAMILY. Canadian Resources on the Family. Ottawa, 1972; revised edition, 1973.
A complete bibliography of Canadian resources dealing with family life.

ADDENDUM

The following items bring the annotations up to December 1974.

BAGUEDOR, Eve. Separation: Journal of a Marriage. New York: Warner Paperback, 1974.
A twenty-year old marriage results in separation. The book describes the progress of the separation.

BOSCO, Antoinette. "When Marriage Ends and Parenthood Remains", Marriage and Family Living, 56 (May 1974), 13-15.
A series of case histories of one-parent family heads.

BRANDWEIN, Ruth A., Carol A. BROWN, and Elizabeth Maury FOX. "Women and Children Last: The Social Situation of Divorced Mothers and their Families", Journal of Marriage and the Family, 36 (August 1974), 489-514.
A review of the literature dealing with the mother-family unit which remains after the father leaves. There appears to be a paucity of research on divorced mothers.

CHILDREN'S BUREAU. One Parent Families. Washington, D.C.: U.S. Dept. of Health. Education and Welfare, 1974, D. HEW Publication No OHD 74-44.
A short booklet dealing with case illustrations of one-parent families. Some guidelines for single parents are included.

CROMWELL, Ronald E., and Joan L. GANGEL. "A Social Action Program Directed to Single Pregnant Girls and Adolescent Girls", The Family Coordinator, XXIII (January 1974), 61-66.

A description of an urban community's action program directed
to single pregnant girls.

CULL, John C. and Richard E. HARDY, eds. Deciding on
 Divorce: Personal and Family Considerations. Springfield,
 Ill.: Charles C. Thomas, 1974.
Ten contributors discuss alternatives to divorce, and post-
divorce counseling.

DAVIS, Hermione G., and Esther FINKEL. "The Single Parent:
 A Growing Challenge to Communal Service", Journal of
 Jewish Communal Service, L (Spring 1974), 251-256.
Casework treatment of single-parent families among a group
of Jewish one-parent families.

EPSTEIN, Joseph. Divorced in America. New York: E. P.
 Dutton, 1974.
A divorced man discusses from first hand experience the
agonies of divorce. He does not hold a great future for the
institution of marriage.

FINER, Morris Sir. Report of the Committee on One-Parent
 Families. London: Her Majesty's Stationery office, 1974,
 2 volumes.
A committee was appointed in England in 1969 to consider the
problems of one-parent families in Great Britain. This extensive report sets out their findings.

GEDDES, Joan Bel. How to Parent Alone: A Guide for Single
 Parents. New York: Seabury Press, 1974.
An advice-type book which attempts to help the single parent
manage his or her family life.

GEGGEL, Elizabeth, and Ruth L. SCHWARTZ. "Helping the
 Single Mother through the Group Process", Journal of Jewish
 Communal Service, L (Spring 1974), 245-250.
Group counseling for one-parent family heads.

HAMILTON, Dorothy. Mindy. Scottdale, Pennsylvania: Herald
 Press, 1973.

A girl attempts to understand her parents' divorce and adjusts
to her new way of life.

HARDY, Richard E., and John C. CULL. Creative Divorce
through Social and Psychological Approaches. Springfield,
Ill.: Charles C. Thomas, 1973.
This book deals with theoretical and practical material related
to the adjustment to divorce.

HERZOG, Elizabeth, and Cecelia E. SUDIA. "Children in
Fatherless Families", in Review of Child Development
Research. Volume 3, edited by Bettye M. Caldwell and
Henry N. Ricciuti, Chicago: University of Chicago Press,
1973, 141-232.
The most comprehensive review of literature on children in
fatherless families in America. The studies under review date
up to 1968.

KELLEHER, Stephen J. Divorce and Remarriage for Catholics.
New York: Doubleday, 1974.
A discussion of these topics related to Catholics.

KEPHART, William M. "Sexual Activities of Divorced Women",
Medical Aspects of Human Sexuality (Can.), IV (September
1974), 10-19.
A discussion of sexuality and divorced women.

LEVINE, Marcia W. "New Family Structures: Challenges to
Family Casework", Journal of Jewish Communal Service,
L (Spring 1974), 238-244.
Work with divorced and reconstituted families.

MARSHALL, Karl A. "Licensing the Minor Unmarried Parent",
Journal of Ontario Children's Aid Societies, 17 (October
1974), 7-9.
A tongue in cheek approach to license teen-age unmarried
mothers. About 54 per cent of teen-age mothers are keeping
their children.

PARKES, Colin Murray. Bereavement: Studies of Grief in Adult Life. New York: International Universities Press, 1972.
The author discusses how widows and widowers react to the experience of bereavement. British and American studies are included in his report.

POLATIN, Phillip and Ellen C. PHILTINE. "Divorce from the Man's View", The Single Parent. 17 (November 1974), 5-10 and p. 38.
Case histories which illustrate how divorce affects the man.

SINGLETON, Mary Ann. Life After Marriage: Divorce as a New Beginning. New York: Stein and Day, 1974.
A practical guide for the divorced woman dealing with the personal growth aspect and realities of post-divorce living.

TREBILCOCK, D. R. "Effects on the Child of Death in the Family", Journal of Ontario Children's Aid Societies, 17 (October 1974), 1-6.
A case history of a young boy whose father died.

WEIGLE, Joan W. "Teaching Child Development to Teenage Mothers", Children Today, III (September -October 1974), 23-25.
A description of a course in child development offered to about 20-25 young girls (average age 15) in the New London public school system in Connecticut.

WEISS, Robert S., ed. Loneliness: The Experience of Emotional and Social Isolation. Cambridge, Mass.: MIT Press, 1973.
Twelve selections discuss loneliness in various forms and at various stages of the life cycle.

WHEELER, Michael. No-Fault Divorce. Boston: Beacon Press, 1974.
An analysis of today's divorce system, and proposals for divorce reform.

151

WILLIAMS, Tannis M. "Childrearing Practices of Young
Mothers", American Journal of Orthopsychiatry, 44
(January 1974), 70-75.
A discussion of childrearing patterns amoung young single
mothers under the age of 20.

APPENDICES

APPENDIX I

THE ONE-PARENT FAMILY IN CANADA:  THE 1971 CENSUS

The 1971 Census indicated that there were 5,070,680 families
in Canada (Statistics Canada, 1971).  There were 478,745 one-
parent families, which comprised 9.44 per cent of all Canadian
families.  Thus, nearly every tenth family is a one-parent
family.

Definition
    The Canadian Census defines a one-parent family as:
        One parent with an unmarried child regardless
        of age, or a man and/or a woman with a
        guardianship child or ward under 21 years of
        age, constitute a family.
    It should also be noted that the family with both husband and
wife present is given the name of "normal family".  The families
with only one parent present are called "broken families".  They
included families whose heads were widowed, divorced, separated for any reasons, or single.
    A one-parent family can be headed by a man or a woman.

Categories of One-Parent Families
    When we speak of one-parent families, we have to consider
that they fall into the following four categories:  widowed,
divorced, separated, and the unmarried mother who keeps her
child.  The 1971 Census gives the following breakdown:

TABLE I
ONE-PARENT FAMILIES IN CANADA: 1971

|  | Male | Female | Total Number of Families | Percent |
|---|---|---|---|---|
| Widowed | 38,070 | 184,555 | 222,625 | 46.6 |
| Divorced | 11,260 | 46,615 | 57,880 | 11.9 |
| Separated | 38,845 | 122,450 | 161,295 | 33.8 |
| Never Married | 12,505 | 24,445 | 36,945 | 7.7 |
|  | 100,680 | 378,065 | 478,745 | 100.0 |

Thus, we find widows constituting nearly half of all one-parent families, the separated, one third and the divorced nearly 12 per cent, while the "never marrieds" cover nearly eight per cent of all families.

Head of One-Parent Families
Table II summarizes the heads of one-parent families in Canada.

TABLE II
HEADS OF ONE-PARENT FAMILIES: CANADA 1971

| Category | Father Only | % | Mother Only | % |
|---|---|---|---|---|
| Separated | 38,845 | 8.11 | 122,450 | 25.58 |
| Widowed | 38,070 | 7.95 | 184,555 | 38.55 |
| Divorced | 11,260 | 2.35 | 46,615 | 9.74 |
| Never Married | 12,205 | 2.61 | 24,445 | 5.11 |
| TOTAL | 100,680 | 21.02 | 378,065 | 78.98 |

In an examination of the facts we notice that 79 per cent of all of one-parent families are headed by a woman and 21 per cent by a man.

The Vital Statistics preliminary annual report (1971) has some data related to one-parent families.

156

In 1971 there were 32,693 illegitimate births, which con-
stituted 9 per cent of all live births. It is estimated that one
half of these children were kept by their mothers to form the
category of the "single parent and her child" (never married).

There were 29,626 divorces in 1971 and 191,324 marriages
during that same year. If we relate marriages to divorce, then
in 1971 for every 6.5 marriages we had one divorce. And so
this category of one-parent families increases. (We had 8.9
marriages per 1,000 population and 137.4 divorces per 100,000
population.)

Quite a few one-parent family heads marry for the second
time. Table III has this data.

An examination of Table III indicates that out of 382,648
men and women who married in 1971 (191,324 marriages), 42,632
married for the second time. Thus, nearly 9 per cent of all
marriages in 1971 included a man or woman who married for
the second time.

TABLE III
SECOND MARRIAGES AND AVERAGE AGE AT SECOND
MARRIAGE IN CANADA, 1971

|  | Number | Average at Marriage* |
|---|---|---|
| Widows | 7,901 | 52.1 |
| Widowers | 6,859 | 57.5 |
| Divorced Women | 14,351 | 35.4 |
| Divorced Men | 15,521 | 39.4 |
| TOTAL | 42,632 | |

*The average age at marriage for single persons was 22.6 years
for brides, and 24.9 years for bridegrooms.

Children in One-Parent Families
Table IV summarizes the number of children aged 0-24
years living in one-parent families in Canada.

157

TABLE IV
CHILDREN IN ONE-PARENT FAMILIES AGES 0-24 AT HOME
1971 CENSUS: CANADA

|  | # Of Families | # Of Children |
|---|---|---|
| Mother Headed: | | |
| Total: | 378,065 | 659,920 |
| Urban: | 314,960 | 541,020 |
| Rural: | 63,100 | 118,905 |
| | | |
| Father Headed: | | |
| Total: | 100,680 | 182,855 |
| Urban: | 74,675 | 131,335 |
| Rural: | 26,005 | 51,520 |
| | | |
| Total Single Parent Families: | | |
| Total: | 478,745 | 842,775 |
| Urban: | 389,635 | 672,355 |
| Rural: | 89,105 | 169,725 |

Average Child Per Family:

| Male Headed: | | Female Headed: | |
|---|---|---|---|
| Total: | 1.816 | Total: | 1.745 |
| Urban: | 1.758 | Urban: | 1.88 |
| Rural: | 1.98 | Rural: | 1.71 |

Canada's population:  21,568,315

Children in 0-24 age group living in single-parent families:
842,775

Percentage of 0-24 age group:  8.5%

APPENDIX II

ONE-PARENT FAMILIES IN THE UNITED STATES
1970-1973

TABLE A
PRIMARY INDIVIDUALS BY MARITAL STATUS,
AGE, AND SEX: 1973 AND 1970

(Numbers in thousands)

| Year and age | Total | Male Married, wife absent | Widowed | Divorced | Single |
|---|---|---|---|---|---|
| **1973** | | | | | |
| All ages | 5,130 | 747 | 1,085 | 1,011 | 2,287 |
| 14 to 34 years | 1,792 | 228 | 5 | 260 | 1,300 |
| 35 to 64 years | 2,023 | 402 | 250 | 625 | 746 |
| 65 years & over | 1,315 | 118 | 830 | 126 | 241 |
| **1970[1]** | | | | | |
| All ages | 4,062 | 545 | 996 | 756 | 1,765 |
| 14 to 34 years | 1,093 | 119 | 6 | 125 | 843 |
| 35 to 64 years | 1,730 | 319 | 240 | 507 | 864 |
| 65 years & over | 1,238 | 108 | 749 | 124 | 258 |
| **Change, 1970 to 1973** | | | | | |
| All ages | 1,068 | 202 | 89 | 255 | 522 |
| 14 to 34 years | 699 | 109 | -1 | 135 | 457 |
| 35 to 64 years | 293 | 83 | 10 | 118 | 82 |
| 65 years & over | 77 | 10 | 81 | 2 | -17 |
| **Female** | | | | | |
| **1973** | | | | | |
| All ages | 8,856 | 517 | 5,423 | 1,002 | 1,914 |
| 14 to 34 years | 1,197 | 100 | 13 | 114 | 972 |
| 35 to 64 years | 3,090 | 294 | 1,532 | 712 | 552 |
| 65 years & over | 4,568 | 123 | 3,878 | 176 | 392 |
| **1970[1]** | | | | | |
| All ages | 7,883 | 516 | 4,915 | 844 | 1,608 |
| 14 to 34 years | 857 | 117 | 3 | 95 | 643 |
| 35 to 64 years | 2,971 | 307 | 1,476 | 598 | 590 |
| 65 years & over | 4,057 | 92 | 3,436 | 152 | 376 |

160

TABLE A continued

| Year and age | Total | Female Married, husband absent | Widowed | Divorced | Single |
|---|---|---|---|---|---|
| Change, 1970 to 1973 | | | | | |
| All ages | 973 | 1 | 508 | 158 | 306 |
| 14 to 34 years | 340 | -17 | 10 | 19 | 329 |
| 35 to 64 years | 119 | -13 | 56 | 114 | -38 |
| 65 years & over | 511 | 31 | 442 | 24 | 16 |

1Revised using population controls based on the 1970 census.

TABLE B

PERSONS UNDER 18 YEARS OLD IN FAMILIES BY PRESENCE AND MARITAL STATUS
OF PARENTS BY RACE: 1973 AND 1970 (Numbers in thousands)

| | 1973 | | | 1970[1] | | | Change, 1970 to 1973 | | |
|---|---|---|---|---|---|---|---|---|---|
| | All races | White | Negro | All races | White | Negro | All races | White | Negro |
| Total persons under 18 in families | 67,520 | 57,125 | 9,432 | 68,685 | 58,429 | 9,325 | -1,165 | -1,304 | 107 |
| Per cent | 100.0 | 100.0 | 100.0 | 100.0 | 100.0 | 100.0 | - | - | - |
| Living with both parents | 82.7 | 87.8 | 52.0 | 85.8 | 90.1 | 59.1 | -3.1 | -2.3 | -7.1 |
| Living with one or neither parent | 17.3 | 12.2 | 48.0 | 14.2 | 9.9 | 40.9 | 3.1 | 2.3 | 7.1 |
| Living with mother only | 13.7 | 9.7 | 38.0 | 10.8 | 7.8 | 29.8 | 2.9 | 1.9 | 8.2 |
| Mother: Single | 1.3 | 0.3 | 7.3 | 0.8 | 0.2 | 4.5 | 0.5 | 0.1 | 2.8 |
| Separated | 4.5 | 2.6 | 16.4 | 3.4 | 1.7 | 13.9 | 1.1 | 0.9 | 2.5 |
| Other married, husband absent | 1.0 | 0.8 | 2.2 | 1.3 | 1.1 | 2.6 | -0.3 | -0.3 | -0.4 |
| Widowed | 2.3 | 1.7 | 5.5 | 2.0 | 1.7 | 4.2 | 0.3 | - | 1.3 |
| Divorced | 4.6 | 4.2 | 6.6 | 3.3 | 3.1 | 4.6 | 1.3 | 1.1 | 2.0 |
| Living with father only | 1.2 | 1.1 | 2.1 | 1.1 | 0.9 | 2.3 | 0.1 | 0.2 | -0.2 |
| Father: Single | - | - | 0.1 | - | - | 0.1 | - | - | - |
| Separated | 0.2 | 0.2 | 0.5 | 0.2 | 0.2 | 0.5 | - | - | - |
| Other married, wife absent | 0.2 | 0.2 | 0.2 | 0.2 | 0.1 | 0.7 | - | 0.1 | -0.5 |
| Widowed | 0.4 | 0.3 | 0.9 | 0.4 | 0.3 | 0.9 | - | - | - |
| Divorced | 0.4 | 0.4 | 0.4 | 0.3 | 0.3 | 0.1 | 0.1 | 0.1 | 0.3 |
| Living with neither parent | 2.4 | 1.5 | 7.9 | 2.3 | 1.2 | 8.8 | 0.1 | 0.3 | -0.9 |

- Represents zero.  R
[1] Revised using population controls based on the 1970 census.

SOURCE: Tables A and B from: Marital Status and Living
        Arrangements, March 1973. Current Population
        Reports, Series P-20, No. 255, November 1973,
        Bureau of Census, U.S. Dept. of Commerce.

TABLE C
ESTIMATED REMARRIAGES AND REMARRIAGE RATES OF
MEN AND WOMEN: UNITED STATES, 1965 TO 1969
(Remarriage rates computed per 1,000 widowed and divorced
men or women 14 years of age and over)

| | Men | | Women | |
|---|---|---|---|---|
| Year | Estimated remarriages | Remarriage rate | Estimated remarriages | Remarriage rate |
| 1969 | 499,000 | 130.9 | 496,000 | 41.3 |
| 1968 | 467,000 | 125.8 | 466,000 | 39.8 |
| 1967 | 439,000 | 123.1 | 437,000 | 37.8 |
| 1966 | 426,000 | 123.0 | 423,000 | 38.1 |
| 1965 | 410,000 | 115.2 | 407,000 | 37.3 |

SOURCE: Tables C and D from: Remarriages: United States.
        DHEW Publication No. HRA 74-1903, December
        1973, Public Health Service, U.S. Department of
        Health, Education and Welfare. Series 21, No. 25.

TABLE D
PER CENT DISTRIBUTION OF MARRIAGES BY PREVIOUS MARITAL STATUS OF BRIDE AND OF GROOM, BY COLOUR: MARRIAGE-REGISTRATION AREA, 1960, 1965, AND 1969

| Colour and previous marital status | 1969 | | 1965 | | 1960 | |
|---|---|---|---|---|---|---|
| | Bride | Groom | Bride | Groom | Bride | Groom |
| White | | | | | | |
| All marriages[1] | 100.0 | 100.0 | 100.0 | 100.0 | 100.0 | 100.0 |
| Single | 75.7 | 75.9 | 79.0 | 78.8 | 79.2 | 80.3 |
| Previously married | 24.3 | 24.1 | 21.0 | 21.2 | 20.8 | 19.7 |
| Widowed | 5.5 | 4.5 | 5.4 | 4.7 | 5.5 | 4.9 |
| Divorced | 18.8 | 19.6 | 15.6 | 16.5 | 15.3 | 14.8 |
| All other | | | | | | |
| All marriages[1] | 100.0 | 100.0 | 100.0 | 100.0 | 100.0 | 100.0 |
| Single | 81.0 | 78.9 | 82.7 | 81.2 | 79.4 | 79.1 |
| Previously married | 19.0 | 21.1 | 17.3 | 18.8 | 20.6 | 20.9 |
| Widowed | 5.0 | 5.2 | 5.6 | 6.2 | 6.4 | 6.8 |
| Divorced | 14.0 | 16.0 | 11.7 | 12.6 | 14.2 | 14.0 |

[1]Includes only marriages for which color and previous marital status were stated.

APPENDIX III

ONE-PARENT FAMILIES IN GREAT BRITAIN

TABLE 1
THE NUMBER OF ONE-PARENT FAMILIES IN
GREAT BRITAIN: APRIL 1971

| Sex and marital status of parent | Number of families | Thousands Number with parent economically active* | Number of children |
|---|---|---|---|
| Female: | | | |
| Single | 49 | 22 | 77 |
| Married | 187 | 85 | 354 |
| Widowed | 131 | 72 | 213 |
| Divorced | 119 | 65 | 235 |
| Total female | 485** | 245** | 879 |
| Male: | | | |
| Single | 11 | 10 | 22 |
| Married | 51 | 49 | 74 |
| Widowed | 33 | 30 | 55 |
| Divorced | 21 | 20 | 36 |
| Total male | 116 | 109 | 187 |
| Grand total | 601 | 354 | 1,066 |

\* "Economically active" means that during census week the person was working, seeking work or waiting to take up a job, or intending to seek work but sick.
\*\* These figures do not show the exact total of the individual items because of "rounding".

165

TABLE II
REVISED ESTIMATES OF THE NUMBER OF ONE-
PARENT FAMILIES IN GREAT BRITIAN:  APRIL 1971

| Sex and marital status of parent | Number of families (thousands) | Percentage in receipt of supplementary benefit | Number of children (thousands) |
|---|---|---|---|
| Female: | | % | |
|   Single | 90 | 68 | 120 |
|   Married | 190 | 54 | 360 |
|   Widowed | 120 | 21 | 200 |
|   Divorced | 120 | 33 | 240 |
| Total | 520 | 44 | 920 |
| Male | 100 | 7 | 160 |
| Grand total | 620 | 38 | 1,080 |

Source of percentage in receipt of supplementary benefit:
Department of Health and Social Security supplementary benefit
statistics.

TABLE III
ESTIMATE OF THE AGE DISTRIBUTION OF LONE PARENTS*

| | Thousands | | | | | |
|---|---|---|---|---|---|---|
| | Fatherless families | | | | | Mother-less families |
| Ages | Single | Married | Widowed | Divorced | All families | |
| All ages** | 90 | 190 | 120 | 120 | 520 | 100 |
| Under 30 | 67 | 75 | 4 | 28 | 174 | 12 |
| 30-44 | 17 | 86 | 46 | 72 | 221 | 46 |
| 45 & over | 6 | 29 | 70 | 20 | 125 | 42 |
| Percentage under 30 | 74.4 | 39.5 | 3.3 | 23.3 | 33.5 | 12.0 |

*The figures are based on the proportionate age distribution as
revealed by the April 1971 census except that:

1.  the additional 40,000 single mothers are assumed to be under 30 years of age;
2.  in reducing the census figures for widows to a total of 120,000 the reduction has been made entirely from the age group 45 and over.

** Very few of the lone parents are over the minimum ages for retirement pension.

TABLE IV
ESTIMATE OF THE AGE DISTRIBUTION OF CHILDREN
IN ONE-PARENT FAMILIES*

| | Thousands | | | | | |
| | Fatherless families | | | | All families | Mother-less families |
| Ages | Single | Married | Widowed | Divorced | | |
|---|---|---|---|---|---|---|
| 0-4 | 70 | 110 | 20 | 40 | 240 | 20 |
| 5-9 | 40 | 140 | 40 | 90 | 310 | 60 |
| 10-14 | 5 | 85 | 90 | 90 | 270 | 60 |
| 15-18 | 5 | 25 | 50 | 20 | 100 | 20 |
| Total | 120 | 360 | 200 | 240 | 920 | 160 |

*These figures are based on the General Household Survey for 1971 and 1972 rated up to agree with the estimate of the number of children in one-parent families at April 1971.

SOURCE: Morris, Finer, Sir. Report of the Committee on One-Parent Families. London: Her Majesty's Stationery office, 1974. The Government Bookshop, HMSO, P.O. Box 569, London SE1 9NH, England. 2 volumes.

APPENDIX IV

REMARRIAGE IN AMERICA:
A GAP IN FAMILY RESEARCH

Benjamin Schlesinger

An examination of family research in 1968 would indicate
clearly that remarriage as a family pattern has, to date,
received little attention by investigators of family life in
North America. To facilitate a review of our knowledge
in this area an "inventory of previous findings" has been
developed by the author.

AN INVENTORY OF FINDINGS ON REMARRIAGE

As a Phenomenon
    (a) A higher number of people in contemporary
America experience plural marriages than in some societies classified as polygamous. (1)
    (b) Whenever there is a high divorce rate, there is a
high remarriage rate. (2)

Statistical Knowledge
    (a) In 1944 in the U.S.A., one out of every eight
brides was married at least once. (3)
    (b) In 1940 for a divorcée of age 30, chances of even-
tual remarriage were 94 out of 100, for a widow of 30
years, 60 out of 100, for a spinster aged 30, 48 out of
100. (4)
    (c) In a study of 14 states in the U.S.A. in 1950, of
brides aged 30-34 years, only half entered first marriage; of brides aged 45-49 years one-fifth entered first
marriage; of brides aged past 60 years less than one-
tenth entered first marriage. (5)

(d) In 1959 in the U.S.A. the median ages at time of marriage were:

|  | males | females |
|---|---|---|
| single | 22.8 | 20.3 |
| second marriage | 38.3 | 34 |
| third marriage | 46.9 | 41.4 |

3 percent of brides and grooms marry a third time. (6)

(e) Data shows that two-thirds of the women and three-fourths of the men who are divorced will remarry. (7)

(f) The elapsed median time prior to remarriage for the divorced is 2.7 years, for widowed 3.5 years. (8)

## Types of Remarriage

(a) There are 8 types of remarriage:

    divorced man - single woman
    divorced man - widowed woman
    divorced man - divorced woman
    single man - divorced woman
    single man - widowed woman
    widowed man - single woman
    widowed man - widowed woman
    widowed man - divorced woman (9)

(b) There are three types of children involved in remarriage:

    father and children and new mother
    mother and children and new father
    father and children and mother and children
    childless

(c) Three-fourths of remarried mothers have custody of children. One-third of remarried fathers have custody of children. (10)

## Social Class Variations

(a) Rate of remarriage is higher among the poorly educated than among people with high school or college education. (11)

## Risks in Remarriage

(a) Lowest percentage of remarriages involves persons who have been previously widowed.

(b) In 1959, of all remarriages in U.S.A., three-quarters were divorced, one-quarter widowed. (12)

(c) One-third of divorced women remarry within one year. Half of divorced women remarry within two years. Two-thirds of divorced women remarry within five years. (13)

Mating Patterns and
Other Factors Related to It

(a) When they remarry, divorced persons are more likely to select mates who have been divorced than they are to choose single or widowed mates. There is similar homogamy in relation to widowed persons. (14)

(b) Second marriages ending in divorce show a shorter duration than first marriages. (15)

(c) Divorced persons are substantially poorer marital risks than the single or widowed. (16)

(d) Remarriages are more likely to end in divorce than are first marriages. (17)

(e) Those who took longer between first serious consideration of the divorce and filing the suit were more likely to remarry early.

(f) When there is a mutual suggestion for divorce, usually 50 percent remarried between 14 months after divorce. If husband suggested divorce, 30 percent remarried after 14 months. If wife suggested divorce, 41 percent remarried after 14 months. (18)

(g) Highest type of remarriage involves one partner who has been divorced previously. The major categories are:

> single man - divorced woman
> two divorced persons
> divorced man - single woman (19)

(h) Divorced persons were fairly good risks for subsequent marriages, and remarriages after widowhood are as happy as first marriages. (20)

(i) Remarried men made lower adjustment scores than remarried women (sample of 47). (21)

Children in Remarriage

(a) Remarriage is not harmful to children. (22)

(b) Adjustment to stepfathers is better than adjustment

to stepmothers.

(c) Children are likely to feel rejected by both natural and stepparent (sample 2, 145 stepchildren). (23)

(d) There is little evidence to support the idea of special problems between stepparents and stepchildren. (24)

(e) Only boys living with their fathers and stepmothers reported liking fewer of their school mates than was true among any other family types. There were no other differences found in adjustment of children in various family types. (25)

## Courtship and Social Life

(a) Remarriages are less likely to be marked by honeymoons, presents, and more likely to be marked by civil rather than religious ceremonies. (26)

(b) The sex adjustment in remarriage binds the pair together more comfortably than in first marriage. (27)

(c) The social life often has to undergo a considerable reorganization.

## Studies in Remarriage

(a) The only extensive study of American remarriage has been done by Jessie Bernard (28)—2,009 cases of remarriage.

(b) Other references usually relate to statistical analyses. (29)

(c) The International Bibliography on Marriage and the Family lists only 19 items directly related to remarriage; of these, 6 are statistical items. The year publication of the items listed is: 1930-1950, 8; 1950-1960, 9; 1960-1964, 2; total 19 items.

## Conclusion

In Canada, we do not have one study on this topic (30), and the United States appears to offer very little in this area. Although we have a small amount of studies related to the One-Parent Family (31), we need now to proceed to examine systematically the next step in family reorganization, namely, remarriage.

References

(1)  Paul H. Landis, "Sequential Marriage," Journal of
     Home Economics, XLII (October 1950), 625-628.
(2)  W. J. Goode, After Divorce (Glencoe: The Free
     Press, 1956).
(3)  Metropolitan Life Insurance, Statistical Bulletin,
     January 1944.
(4)  Ibid., May 1945.
(5)  Ibid., May 1950.
(6)  Vital Statistics of the United States, Marriage and
     Divorce Statistics, 1959, Section 2, p. 9.
(7)  Paul C. Glick, American Families (New York: John
     Wiley and Sons, 1957), p. 139.
(8)  Ibid., pp. 138-139.
(9)  George Simpson, People in Families (New York:
     Thomas Y. Crowell, 1960), p. 386.
(10) Jessie Bernard, Remarriage (New York: The Dryden
     Press, 1956), p. 212.
(11) P. C. Glick, and H. Carter, "Marriage Patterns
     and Educational Level," American Sociological
     Review, XXIII (1958), 294-300.
(12) "Trends in Divorce and Family Disruption," Health,
     Education, and Welfare Indicators, XXIV (August
     1963), 14.
(13) Paul H. Jacobson, American Marriage and Divorce
     (New York: Holt, Rinehart and Winston, 1959),
     pp. 69-70.
(14) Thomas P. Monahan, "The Changing Nature and In-
     stability of Remarriages," Eugenics Quarterly,
     V (June 1950), 73-85.
(15) Thomas P. Monahan, "The Duration of Marriage to
     Divorce: Second Marriages and Migratory Types,"
     Marriage and Family Living, XXI (May 1959),
     134-138.
(16) Bureau of the Census, Current Population Reports,
     Series P-20, No. 23, March 4, 1949.
(17) Thomas P. Monahan, "How Stable are Remar-
     riages?," American Journal of Sociology, LVIII
     (November 1952), 280-288.
(18) W. J. Goode, op. cit.

(19) Charles E. Bowerman, "Assortative Mating by Previous Marital Status; Seattle, 1939-1946," American Sociological Review, XVIII (April 1953), 171.

(20) Harvey J. Locke, Predicting Adjustment in Marriage (New York: Henry Holt, 1951), pp. 298-309.

(21) Harvey J. Locke, and William J. Klausner, "Marital Adjustment of Divorced Persons in Subsequent Marriage," Sociology and Social Research, XXXIII (November 1948), 97-101.

(22) Jessie Bernard, op. cit.

(23) Charles E. Bowerman, and Donald P. Irish, "Some Relationships of Stepchildren to Their Parents," Marriage and Family Living, XXIV (May 1962), 113-121.

(24) F. Ivan Nye, "Child Adjustment in Broken and in Unhappy Unbroken Homes," Marriage and Family Living, XIX (November 1957), 356-361.

(25) Lee G. Burchinal, "Characteristics of Adolescents from Unbroken, Broken, and Reconstituted Families," Journal of Marriage and the Family, XXVI (February 1946), 44-51.

(26) August B. Hollingshead, "Marital Status and Wedding Behavior," Marriage and Family Living, XIV (November 1952), 308-311.

(27) Gerald R. Leslie, The Family in Social Context (London: Oxford University Press, 1967), pp. 651-652.

(28) Jessie Bernard, op. cit.

(29) Joan Aldous, and Reuben Hill, International Bibliography of Research in Marriage and the Family (Minneapolis: University of Minnesota Press, 1967), p. 158.

(30) Frederick Elkin, The Family in Canada (Ottawa: Canadian Conference on the Family, 1964).
John Spencer, An Inventory of Family Research and Studies in Canada (1963-1967) (Ottawa: Vanier Institute of the Family, 1967).

(31) Benjamin Schlesinger, "The One-Parent Family: Recent Literature," Journal of Marriage and the Family, XXVIII (February 1966), 103-109.
"The One-Parent Family: An Overview," Family Life Coordinator, VI (Part I, October 1966), 133-139.

APPENDIX V

## ADDRESSES OF PUBLISHERS

Abingdon Press,
201 Eight Ave.,
Nashville, Tenn. 37202

Abraxas Corporation,
874 Malcolm Ave.,
Los Angeles, Calif. 90024

Aldine-Atherton,
529 South Wabash Ave.,
Chicago, Ill. 60605

Allyn and Bacon,
470 Atlantic Ave.,
Boston, Mass. 02110

Appleton-Century-Crofts,
446 Park Ave. S.,
New York, N.Y. 10016

Association Press,
291 Broadway,
New York, N.Y. 10016

Bantam Books,
666 Fifty Ave.,
New York, N.Y. 10019

Barnes and Noble,
105 Fifth Ave.,
New York, N.Y. 10013

Beacon Press,
25 Beacon St.,
Boston, Mass. 02108

Bobbs-Merrill Co.,
4300 63rd St.,
Indianapolis, Ind. 46206

Burns and MacEachern,
62 Railside Rd.,
Don Mills, Ontario

Canadian Council on Social
  Development,
55 Parkdale Ave.,
Ottawa, Ontario K1Y 1E5

Chandler Publishing Co.,
604 Mission St.,
San Francisco, Calif. 94105

Child Welfare League of America,
67 Irving Place,
New York, N.Y. 10003

Child Welfare League of
America, Consortium on
Early Childbearing and
Childrearing, Suite 618
1145 - 19th St., N. W.,
Washington, D. C. 20036

Collier Books,
Front and Brown Streets,
Riverside, N. J. 08075

Columbia University Press,
136 South Broadway,
Irvington, N. Y. 10533

Thomas Y. Crowell,
201 Park Ave. S.,
New York, N. Y. 10003

Deseret Book Co.,
P. O. Box 958
Salt Lake City, Utah 84110

Dodd, Mead and Co.,
79 Madison Ave.,
New York, N. Y. 10016

Dorsey Press,
1818 Ridge Road
Homewood, Ill. 60430

Doubleday and Co.,
Garden City,
New York, N. Y. 11530

Dryden Press,
901 No. Elm,
Hinsdale, Ill. 60521

M. Evans and Co.,
216 East 49th St.,
New York, N. Y. 10017

Family and Children's Services
of London and Middlesex,
P. O. Box 848
London, Ontario

Family Service Association
of America,
44 East 23rd St.,
New York, N. Y. 10010

Arthur Fields Books,
201 Park Ave. S.,
New York, N. Y. 10003

Fortress Press,
2900 Queens Lane
Pennsylvania, Pa. 19129

Funk and Wagnalls,
380 Madison Ave.,
New York, N. Y. 10017

General Learning Press,
Box 2345,
Morristown, N. J. 07960

Glendessary Press, Inc.,
2512 Grove St.,
Berkeley, Calif. 94704

Graded Press,
201 - 8th Ave. S.,
Nashville, Tenn. 37202

Grune and Stratton,
381 Park Ave. S.,
New York, N.Y. 10016

Harcourt, Brace and
  Jovanovich,
757 Fifth Ave.,
New York, N.Y. 10017

Harper and Row,
49 E. 33rd St.,
New York, N.Y. 10016

Hart Publishing Co.,
510 Sixth Ave.,
New York, N.Y. 10010

Harvard University Press,
Cambridge, Mass. 02138

Herald Press,
Scottsdale, Pa. 15683

Herder and Herder,
252 Madison Ave.,
New York, N.Y. 10016

Holt, Rinehard and Winston,
383 Madison Ave.,
New York, N.Y. 10017

Houghton-Mifflin,
110 Tremart St.,
Boston, Mass. 02107

Humanities Press,
303 Park Ave. S.,
New York, N.Y. 10010

Information Canada,
171 Slater St.,
Ottawa, Ontario K1A 0S9

Iowa State University Press,
Press Building,
Ames, Iowa 50010

Michael Joseph,
26 Bloomsbury St.,
London WC1, England

Jossey-Bass,
615 Montgonery St.,
San Francisco, Calif. 94111

KTAV Publishing House,
120 E. Broadway,
New York, N.Y. 10002

Alfred A. Knopf,
501 Madison Ave.,
New York, N.Y. 10022

John Knox Press,
801 East Main St.,
Richmond, Va. 23209

Lippincott, J.B.,
East Washington Square,
Philadelphia, Pa. 19105

Little, Brown and Co.,
34 Beacon St.,
Boston, Mass. 02106

Macmillan Co.,
866 Third Ave.,
New York, N.Y. 10022

Markham Publishing,
3322 West Peterson Ave.,
Chicago, Ill. 60645

McGraw-Hill,
1221 Avenue of the Americas,
New York, N. Y. 10017

McGraw-Hill Ryerson,
330 Progress Ave.,
Scarborough, Ontario

McKay, David,
750 Third Ave.,
New York, N. Y. 10017

Messner, Julian,
8 West 40th St.,
New York, N. Y. 10018

Methodist Church, Board of
 Education,
P. O. Box 871,
Nashville, Tenn. 37202

Minnesota Council on
 Family Relations,
1219 University Ave. S. E.,
Minneapolis, Minn. 55414

William Morrow and Co.,
105 Madison Ave.,
New York, N. Y. 10016

Mothers in Action,
Munro House,
9 Poland St.,
London W1, England

National Association of Social
 Workers,
2 Park Ave.,
New York, N. Y. 10016

National Council on Family
 Relations,
1219 University Ave. S. E.,
Minneapolis, Minn. 55414

National Council on Jewish Women,
1 West 47th St.,
New York, N. Y. 10036

National Council on Illegitimacy,
44 East 23rd St.,
New York, N. Y. 10010

Thomas Nelson and Sons,
Copewood and Davis Streets,
Camden, N. J. 08103

New Press,
56 The Esplanade East,
Toronto, Ontario

Newman Press,
400 Sette Dr.,
Paramus, N. J. 07652

Odyssey Press,
850 Third Ave.,
New York, N. Y. 10022

Oxford University Press,
200 Madison Ave.,
New York, N. Y. 10016

Paulist Press,
400 Sette Dr.,
Paramus, N.J. 07652

F. E. Peacock Publishers,
401 West Irving Park Rd.,
Itasen, Ill. 60143

Penguin Books,
7110 Ambassador Rd.,
Baltimore, Md. 21207

Pocket Books, Inc.,
630 Fifth Ave.,
New York, N.Y. 10020

Prentice-Hall,
Englewood Cliffs, N.J.
07632

Public Affairs Committee,
381 Park Ave. S.,
New York, N.Y. 10016

G. P. Putnam's Sons Inc.,
200 Madison Ave.,
New York, N.Y. 10016

Rand McNally & Co.,
Box 7600,
Chicago, Ill. 60680

Random House,
201 East 50th St.,
New York, N.Y. 10022

Henry Regnery Co.,
114 W. Illinois St.,
Chicago, Ill. 60610

Ronald Press,
79 Madison Ave.,
New York, N.Y. 10016

Routledge & Kegan Paul,
68-74 Carter Lane,
London EC4, England

Russell Sage Foundation,
230 Park Ave.,
New York, N.Y. 10017

Simon and Schuster,
630 Fifth Ave.,
New York, N.Y. 10020

Scott, Foresman and Co.,
1900 East Lake Ave.,
Glenview, Ill. 60025

Charles Scribner's Sons,
597 Fifth Ave.,
New York, N.Y. 10017

The Single Parent, Parents
  Without Partners,
7910 Woodmont Ave.,
Washington, D.C. 20014

Southern Illinois University Press,
600 West Grand,
Carbondale, Ill. 62903

Springer Publishing Co.,
200 Park Ave. S.,
New York, N.Y. 10003

St. Martin's Press,
175 Fifth Ave.,
New York, N.Y. 10010

Steirman Communications,
545 Madison Ave.,
New York, N. Y. 10022

Charles C. Thomas,
301-327 E. Lawrence Ave.,
Springfield, Ill. 62717

Transactional Analysts
1005 Dunn Rd.,
St. Louis, Miss. 63031

United Nations Publications,
United Nations Sales Section,
New York, N. Y.

University of Chicago Press,
5801 Ellis Ave.,
Chicago, Ill. 60637

University of Toronto Press,
Toronto, Ontario M5S 1A6

Vanier Institute of the Family,
151 Slater St.,
Ottawa, Ontario K1P 5H3

Viking Press,
625 Madison Ave.,
New York, N. Y. 10022

Wadsworth Publishing Co.,
Belmont, Calif. 94002

Westminster Press,
925 Witherspoon Building,
Philadelphia, Pa. 19107

John Wiley and Sons,
850 3rd Ave.,
New York, N. Y. 10016

Yale University Press,
92A Yale Station,
New Haven, Conn. 06520

# AUTHOR INDEX

Abrahams, R. B.  144
Abrascas Corporation  129
Ackerman, N. J.  144
Ackerman, N. W.  129
Adams, B. N.  114
Adams, P. L.  120, 124
Agree, R. H.  144
Aldous, J.  112
Anderson, M.  114
Anderson, W. T.  114
Andrews, R. O.  63
Anshen, R. N.  63
Arlen, M. J.  129
Bach, G. R.  83
Baer, J.  136
Baguedor, E.  139, 148
Bahr, H. M.  145
Baizerman, M.  140
Bales, R. E.  71
Bartemeier, L.  63
Bartlett, C. J.  97
Beck, F.  97
Becker, H.  97
Bell, N. W.  64
Bell, R. R.  63, 73, 74, 113
Bellin, S. S.  77
Benson, L.  114
Berardo, F. M.  71, 98, 118, 145
Bergler, E.  87

Bernard, J.  87, 110, 114
Bernard, S. E.  74
Bernstein, N. R.  87
Bernstein, R.  104, 140
Bigner, J. J.  120
Billingsley, A.  115
Bitterman, C. M.  110
Blake, P.  120
Block, J. L.  129
Blood, R. O.  120
Blumenthal, R. D.  139
Boalt, G.  64
Bogatta, M. L.  117
Bohanan, P.  129
Boll, E. S.  64
Borgatta, E. F.  106
Bosco, A.  148
Bossard, J. H. S.  64
Bowerman, C. E.  104, 110
Brailey, F. W. L.  88
Brandwein, R. A.  148
Briscoe, W. C.  129
Broderick, C. E.  114
Brown, C. A.  148
Burchinal, L. G.  88
Burgess, E. W.  64, 65
Burgess, J. K.  120
Burton, R. V.  74
Cain, A. C.  110
Canada. Dominion Bureau of Statistics  74

180

183

184